just PARENTiNG

just PARENTING

CHRISTINE WRIGHT

Scripture Union
130 City Road, London EC1V 2NJ

© Christine Wright 1994
First published 1995

ISBN 0 86201 960 5

Unless otherwise specified, Scripture quotations in this publication are
from the Good News Bible, Copyright New Testament © American Bible
Society, New York, 1966, 1971, and 4th edition 1976. Old Testament
© American Bible Society, New York, 1976. Published by The Bible
Societies, Collins/Fontana.

British Library Cataloguing-in-Publication Data.
A catalogue record for this book is available from the British Library.

Cover design by Ross Advertising & Design, Buckinghamshire.
Cover illustration and book illustrations by Taffy Davies.

Phototypeset by Intype, London.
Printed and bound in Great Britain by Cox and Wyman Ltd, Reading,
Berkshire.

To those who were 'just parents' to me,
Alan and Eileen

Contents

Preface   9
1   The biggest change you'll ever make!   11
2   Waiting days   19
3   'There's nobody quite like me'   27
4   The big event   35
5   Early days   45
6   Small world, isn't it?   53
7   On the move   61
8   No two are the same   69
9   Moulding the clay   79
10 Standards of play   91
11 Three-legged stools   101
12 The intruder   109
13 Just parents   117

Preface

Just Parenting is for people awaiting the birth of a child or with children under the age of five. I know that parents bringing up children can feel daunted by the magnitude of their task. There are many skills to learn and great responsibilities. One of the areas that concerns many of us is how to help children develop spiritually, but most child-care books do not mention this at all.

How, in fact, do children learn about God? How much are they influenced by the atmosphere of their home, by the example we set and the things we teach, either consciously or unconsciously? What do they absorb at church and from the local community?

There are no easy, obvious answers to these questions, but I hope that this book will help you think through the issues and come to your own conclusions. God calls us to be *just* parents, which means taking time to reflect on what we are doing.

I offer you *Just Parenting* as a tool. I hope that it will help you make your family life more enjoyable and satisfying.

Christine Wright

1

The biggest change you'll ever make!

Meet Tom and Kath. No, they're not real people in the sense that you will ever meet them personally. On the other hand, they *are* real because what they are experiencing is happening to millions of people right now.

Tom and Kath are expecting their first baby. Perhaps their story, which is based on things that have happened to me, my family and my acquaintances, will help you. It will not give you all the answers and is certainly not intended to be a step-by-step guide to baby and child-care. It may give you, whether you read it alone or with your partner, an idea of what it's like to be a parent. It may also suggest ways of bringing up children which could be helpful to you, whether you're expecting your first baby or whether you're further along the track and your child is already born.

Most of all, I hope you will discover ways of enjoying the next few years. Bringing up children can be exhausting and mundane, but there is no reason why it should not be enjoyable too. This is what Tom and Kath are about to discover.

Expecting

Kath is pregnant. Both she and Tom are very pleased because they planned to have a baby. Their families are also happy, especially Kath's mother who adores babies and regrets that she only had one herself. But Tom's parents are not sure that having a baby is such a good idea just at the moment. They feel that the couple should be more secure financially first (and are maybe a little young).

Yet, although it is the very thing both Kath and Tom wanted and have waited for, a few doubts have begun to creep into their minds. I'm sure this isn't uncommon!

We have probably met parents whose lives are dominated by their unruly and demanding offspring, or those who don't even seem to like their children and who just can't wait for them to grow up. While we say to ourselves, 'That couldn't possibly happen to us,' there's always a secret fear that our children will turn out to be impossible to handle and that we will be disgraced in front of everyone.

On the other hand, when we meet happy, well-behaved children, whose parents look as though they were born to be good mothers or fathers, we think, 'I'll never make the grade. I don't think I've got the gift for it.'

It's rather like seeing musicians give effortless performances that make you think that they were born able to play to concert standard. You forget the dedication, the hours of practice they've put in when they could have been out playing ball or sitting slumped in front of the television.

And so it is with being a parent. Nobody is born a good parent: it does take practice and dedication. And, yes, some people may be better at the job than others. That's inevitable, just as some of us are always going to be better musicians than others. However, I'm sure it's equally true that everyone has the capability to be an *adequate* parent. We may not manage this alone, without advice or help and without making any blunders. But you wouldn't expect anyone learning a new skill or job to become proficient, just like that!

Tom's view of being a father

Tom is particularly anxious about his ability to be a good father. His parents were, in his eyes, very competent. They always seemed to be in control. They made rules and expected him and his sister to keep them. They always knew what to do in every situation and never appeared to have a moment's doubt about any decision they made. So Tom grew up with a feeling of anxiety about his own ability to make decisions wisely. His parents rarely gave him a chance to try out his own ideas and, when they did, Tom always had the impression that they were secretly hoping he would fail so that he would see how much better it was to follow their advice.

The truth is that, deep inside, Tom still feels like a little boy, despite the fact that he is married and has a job. His parents' disapproval of the timing of Kath's pregnancy makes him uneasy and gives him a nagging sense of guilt. And all this adds to his fear that he won't be able to make the grade as a dad.

Consider three possible solutions for Tom.

1 He might try to live up to his childhood idea of a good father. When the baby is born, he might repeat the pattern passed on to him by his own family. He could become a controlling parent. If he ever felt any doubt about the best thing to do in any situation, he wouldn't show it. If the outcome were bad, he would make sure that someone else took the blame. ('I told you it would be a mistake. You should have done it my way, then everything would have turned out well.') In this way (if he got away with it) he could prevent anyone ever discovering his feeling of inadequacy and fear of making mistakes.

2 He could react against his upbringing and treat his children in a totally different way. Instead of controlling them, he would allow his sons or daughters to do anything they liked. Just as his parents denied him certain things ('for his own good'), he would indulge his children and let them have everything he could afford. It would be his way of trying to make up for what happened to him – a way of compensating for the coldness that he sometimes experienced himself as a child.

3 He might take the opportunity to think through his concept of a 'good parent'. This involves a degree of pain for Tom since he loves his parents and finds it difficult to admit that they made mistakes; but it is a good thing for him to take this further step of growing up now that he is to have a child himself.

He needs to face the fact that his parents might have been wrong to control his life so tightly. He must see that it would have been better for him to have been given as much responsibility as he could handle. That means genuine opportunities to make his own decisions, depending on his age (for instance, which shoes to wear when he was three; how to spend his pocket money when he was eight).

However, it's equally important to recognise the strength of his parents' care and protection when he was small and vulnerable. He can be truly grateful to them for that.

So, Tom needs to search for a balance that he will find comfortable for his own parenting style.

Kath's view of being a mother

Kath never really worries about anything for long, but her expectations of family life are very different from Tom's. She never knew her father, but always had a good relationship with her mother who was very easy-going and affectionate. Their home was always full of half-finished projects, piles of clothes waiting to be ironed or mended, discarded books, magazines and other stuff.

Her mother's life was full and Kath had to fit her needs around her mother's hectic schedule. Because of that experience, she assumes that having a child will have very little impact on her present life. She intends to return to work shortly after the baby's birth and she assumes that she and Tom will be able to take the child with them wherever they go, so that neither their social lives nor their work will be much affected.

Perhaps she has forgotten her own childhood anger at times when she was interrupted in the middle of an absorbing game to 'dash out shopping' or 'go and meet some friends', or her sadness at always being the last to be picked up from school.

As a child, Kath was powerless to change the way things were done in the family and she had to learn to bury her feelings about what was happening to her.

Of course, she loved her mother and there is much about her childhood to thank her for, but Kath does need to think about whether she wants to treat her children in the same way, if she is to avoid hurting them as she was hurt.

This doesn't imply that Kath should necessarily decide not to return to work after the birth of her baby. There are plenty of good reasons why mothers work and not all of them are to do with money. However, there are more fundamental questions that Kath needs to consider:

1 Is she going, unconsciously, to copy the pattern of her childhood family?

2 Is she going to react against it and do exactly the opposite?

3 Is she going to take the 'growing up' route and mix the best from her mother's ways of doing things with her own conscious decisions about how to bring up her own family?

Talking it out

Most parents do a reasonably good job. We certainly do the best we know how. And there is no reason for rejecting everything our parents did because they made a few mistakes along the way.

Both Tom and Kath will find, when the baby is born, that they have absorbed a great deal about how to care for a child without realising it. But this is *their* family and, although they will draw on what they already know and on other people's advice, what they really have to work out is what sort of parents *they* want to be.

They may be able to do this together or to find others in the same situation who will be willing to work with them. The vital thing for them is to find the time to do the *thinking*. For their baby's sake, let's hope they make it a priority.

An example of a good parent

The idea of God as a parent is centuries old, but it is one that many people find helpful. The Bible tells the story of how God revealed himself as a parent − not prone to mistakes as we are, but the perfect parent, the one we always dreamt of having. He relates to people in just the same ways as mothers or fathers want to relate to their children. He is:

- always devoted to our best interests
- provides all we need, but not always all we want
- protective, but gives opportunities for us to face as much adventure and danger as we can safely handle
- gives guidance, pointing out what we *can* do as well as what we *shouldn't*
- nurturing, but not over-indulgent
- loving
- consistent
- totally just and surprisingly merciful

Are these qualities that parents today aspire to have?

REFLECTION

When I am born, I want to have parents who think big. I don't mind if they don't always get it right, if they fail to be what they set out to be. But don't let them be small-minded or unthinking. I want parents who are full of hope, who keep trying, who believe in themselves. Otherwise, how will I ever learn to be what I was meant to be?

2

Waiting days

With only weeks to go before the birth of the baby, Tom has problems. So much has changed at home recently that he finds it hard to keep up. And he has to admit to himself that he feels jealous of all the attention Kath is getting. Her problems are obvious (and he doesn't envy her those!), but why doesn't anyone realise what he's going through? Nobody is talking about it, so he assumes that he's the only father-to-be who ever felt this way!

Sympathy is often given to the mother-to-be because she is the one who has her whole life changed by the baby, including her physical shape, her sleeping patterns and the hormones that affect her moods and her body. She is the one who must carry round additional and ever-growing weight and who finds, as the pregnancy lengthens, that she may be able to do less and less of what she wants.

A difficult time for Tom

Let's not forget that the father-to-be is also experiencing changes, though less noticeably. Tom is lucky because he has a job, but somehow he feels much less secure. With Kath not working for a while, it seems much more important that he remains in work and there are a lot of new expenses to face. He never realised before how much having a baby could cost! He finds himself thinking more and more about the financial side of things and the responsibility of having to provide for the family year after year. When there were just the two of them, money wasn't really much of an issue, even though they were not that well off. Now it suddenly seems a terrible burden to Tom.

But Kath is not talking much about money at all. Earlier in the pregnancy, she had worried about how they would get by on one salary (and about losing her financial independence when leaving work). Recently, though, she seems to think and speak about nothing but the baby and the progress of her pregnancy. She listens while Tom talks about how they are going to manage financially if she decides not to return to work, but he can tell that she's not at all interested in the subject. Before long, she begins to talk about how the baby is kicking her and how Gita, their neighbour, who is also pregnant, has high blood pressure and has to have hospital rest, and wouldn't it be terrible if that happened to her?

He also notices changes in her behaviour. She has never been house-proud, but suddenly she has become obsessed about keeping the place tidy – no more leaving the washing-up until the morning or spreading newspapers over the furniture!

She sometimes rejects his sexual advances too and never approaches him any more. He can't help feeling pushed aside.

Why is it happening?

It's not stupid or selfish of Tom to feel hurt and alone at this time. Only a few weeks ago, he and Kath were sharing a family life which consisted of two people. They argued and fought, just as every couple is bound to do, but most of the time they were happy whether they were alone together or in company. They were often apart, of course, but when they were together, their focus was on each other. They thought about *our* home, *our* night out or *our* shopping trip. 'Our' meant 'us two'. That is what marriage meant to them – not 'me' and 'you' any longer, but 'us two'.

Now, it's changed. And Kath has become aware of the change more quickly because she's the one whose physical body is more intimately involved. 'Us two' has become 'us three'. Just as Kath focused on Tom at the beginning of their relationship – probably to the virtual exclusion of all other human beings – in the period of 'falling in love' or bonding to the other person, she is now 'falling in love' or bonding with her baby, even before he is born.

Her physical condition is assisting this process because she is aware of the baby every time she moves in that new awkward way. When she walks, she adapts her gait because of the bump and she even lies awake at night because the baby is moving about or making her uncomfortable. It's not the same for Tom who can go for hours at work without giving the baby a single thought.

Kath's focus on the baby affects everything she does. Deep within her is a desire to have the best for the baby. There's no way that she can afford all the things she would like to buy, but she is trying, almost unconsciously, to make the home as perfect as she can for the baby, hence her irritation even with Tom's slight untidiness.

And though Tom sees her lack of interest in sex as a rejection of him, it may not be so. Kath's life is changing very rapidly and the demands on her, both physically and emotionally, are enormous. She still loves Tom, but for a time her love may be expressed in different ways while she is devoting herself entirely and passionately to his baby.

21

It is possible, also, that Kath's temporary indifference to sex is her body's natural way of seeking to protect the baby and ensure his survival.

Mutual understanding

If Kath fails to understand Tom and if he fails to understand her, the couple are heading for trouble!

He thinks she's rejecting him and that he is permanently on the sidelines of her life. Although he may try to be reasonable, he may *feel* like a husband whose wife has another man.

Kath is undergoing profound changes, far deeper than the merely physical. It's hard for her to see things from Tom's point of view and to be patient while he makes his slower, but no less profound, adjustments to his new role. And, while she is focusing mainly on the short-term, about her baby now and when he is born, Tom is thinking more about the long term and the years of commitment that he is facing.

Perhaps this difficult time may be excellent training for parenthood. When the baby is born, Tom and Kath will both have to discover how to put their own needs on one side and think exclusively of what someone else, their demanding baby, needs!

Before the birth, if things are to proceed smoothly, the couple have to be patient with each other. Kath may need to listen seriously to what Tom wants to say about his preoccupation and Tom may need to try to enter more into Kath's immediate interest in herself and her baby. Kath may need to be more sensitive to Tom's sexual needs and Tom may need to be more aware of Kath's greater need for personal privacy. Both should remember that this stage will pass! True, things will never be the same as they were before, but obviously pregnancy itself doesn't last forever. It is a very special time when a great miracle is taking place. It would be strange indeed if Kath and Tom were able to carry on just as before while all this was happening to them.

A great opportunity for men!

Probably it is Tom who will have to make the more conscious adjustments because what is happening to Kath is at a more primal level. If Tom is able to overcome his instinctive personal feelings at this stage, he can achieve something good and positive for the future of his marriage and for the child about to be born.

He can say to himself, 'Yes, I do feel hurt that Kath is not giving me the attention that she used to and seems more concerned with the baby than with me. But I am an adult and, for a while, I can put my feelings on one side. I don't *need* Kath to prove that she loves me all the time, but my baby does need her full attention just now. I'll do my share by supporting her while she's doing this for my baby and take my part in the baby's life by devoting my full attention to the needs of my wife and my child.'

This won't mean that he will stop going to work and give up any roles he has within the church and community. It will mean, however, that whatever he is doing, he will have his family in mind. He won't be focusing on his own needs and desires, but on Kath and the baby.

To be selfless in this way is very hard to achieve. It requires courage and determination because it's much easier to take the coward's way out and leave the woman to get on with the problems of pregnancy. Sadly, despite some progress recently, this kind of abandonment is often still seen in our society as 'macho' or as a man's right. But all of us, whether male or female, need to develop the ability to see things from other people's point of view. This may mean putting our own needs and desires on one side for the moment. Society does not value the concept of self-sacrifice very highly, but it is the example of Jesus, and it is the foundation stone of family life. On it we can build contented and peaceful families.

REFLECTION

'Husbands, love your wives, just as Christ loved the church and gave himself up for her . . . In this same way, husbands ought to love their wives as their own bodies. He who loves his wife loves himself.'
Ephesians 5:25, 28 NIV

Why is this particularly relevant during pregnancy?

3

'There's nobody quite like me'

When Kath has her regular check-ups, she has the privilege of hearing her baby's heart beating. It's something that gives her a thrill every time. It means that her baby is alive and active – a real human being. When we're as involved in the emergence of new life as intimately as Kath is, that fact excites and amazes us, just as it seems mundane and obvious to people who are not!

One of the things that Tom and Kath have discussed is how to bring up their child 'in the right way'. For them, as Christians, the most important thing is that their baby will grow up to know and follow Jesus Christ. They came to faith themselves after leaving school and neither of them has experience of being brought up in a Christian home. This makes them rather anxious about getting things right.

The vast majority of parents, like Kath and Tom, are concerned that their children grow up to be decent, moral people. Most want to pass on spiritual values too, and strive to make sure that their children know about God. They might tell them Bible stories, take them to church or teach them simple prayers. Tom and Kath intend to do

all these things for their children, but they are beginning to wonder if it is enough.

Let's pay a visit to their baby and, in our imagination, try to see things from his point of view. How is he going to learn about God?

'I am myself'

Tom and Kath's baby is very much a part of them. He is still physically attached to his mother and it would be impossible to say where Kath ends and the baby begins. Even after his birth, when the umbilical cord is cut, he will continue to have very strong attachments to his family for many years, probably for the rest of his life.

Those links are vital for his well–being and are a God-given means of ensuring his nurture in the safety of warm, loving relationships. In a very real sense, the baby belongs to Tom and Kath and to the rest of their extended family.

In another sense, he does *not* belong to them. He is not their property. He is a gift to them from God, but a gift they have to treat responsibly, not one they can use in any way that pleases them.

The first thing that Tom and Kath can get 'right' is to free the baby to be himself. He is a unique human being with his own right to be and to do. Of course, it is easy for us as parents to know this in theory while at the same time loading our children with our own baggage – our own dreams and aspirations, the leftovers from our own childhood.

Aspirations

Tom always wanted to be a doctor, but he discovered that he was not quite clever enough. Although he studied as hard as he could, he couldn't make the grade. He found another career, but still wishes that he had had the chance

29

to do what he really wanted.

Would it be right for him to push his children into medicine, even though they have their own aspirations? Put like that, it would seem fairly obvious that Tom should not force his children into careers in which they aren't interested, but how many parents hope that their own dreams will be fulfilled through their children? They may pay for dancing or music lessons, hoping that their off-spring will achieve success where they themselves failed. They might push their sons or daughters into sporting activities or coax them to learn chess or computing skills in order that they might bathe in their children's hoped-for glory.

Some children do have a genuine interest in the same things that fire their parents' imaginations. And then it does no harm to encourage them to succeed. What is important, however, is to be aware of the danger of hi-jacking the child's individual right to be himself or herself, to dream his own dreams, to work for his own aspirations.

Giving them liberty

The baby, as yet unborn, is himself – not a vehicle to boost someone's ego, not a prop to hold up a shaky marriage, not a means of proving anything to the world, not a substitute for another adult's love, not a human 'teddy bear' to be loved to death one moment and discarded the next.

Parents must be unselfish and self-denying because, in the end, our purpose is to become redundant. One day, we will find that our children are self-reliant and don't need us any more. Then we'll know that we have done our work well. Of course, they may want us and love us, and we may need *them* as we grow old or infirm, but we must acknowledge that they are no longer dependent on us.

It *will* be very rewarding and fulfilling to be parents and there will be plenty of joy and fun. It is just as well, though, to remember, even before babies are born, that they will have their own lives to live. One of the best gifts we can give them is the liberty to do just that.

The reality of God

Tom and Kath's baby has an individual personality, and this is also true of God. The great mystery of the Christian faith is that God can know every single person as a unique human being; but more than that, he can have a relationship with each one.

God has known this baby from the very start. It makes sense that he is, even now, communicating with the baby in the womb. The child has not had to wait until he is old enough to understand about God and about what Jesus has done to make it possible to know God. Already, God is reaching out to the child, surrounding him with love, making himself known.

It will be a long time before the baby can understand words or form ideas, so it is clear that God is not communicating verbally. He is not saying endlessly, 'I love you', hoping that the baby will take the message in mentally.

No, his message comes in the way the infant can understand. At peace in his safe environment, the baby has all that he needs. He is comfortable and secure. He is receiving signals of love from his parents as they tailor their movements, their speech and their moods to his presence. This doesn't mean that the baby will be damaged by sudden movements, occasional rows or the unhappy moods of those around him. It does mean, however, that, during the months he is growing inside, the baby will become more and more aware of the general atmosphere into which he is to be born.

As his parents love him, talk to him gently and accept

31

his presence, they are 'speaking' to him about God's love. The same is true even if the parents don't believe in God or don't have a very strong faith. For Tom and Kath as believers, of course, there is a wonderful, added dimension. They can pray for their baby and imagine him surrounded by God's love and care. They can think of their newly enlarged family as part of God's purpose. They can know that, whatever happens to them in the next weeks, months and years, they will be at the centre of God's loving attention.

Spiritual growth

Even before birth, the reality of God surrounds the baby. He is receiving God's love in the way God intended – through the security of the womb and the loving acceptance of his parents. He cannot as yet express or describe that love. He does experience it, however, and the experience of love and acceptance forms the most vital foundation of his physical, mental and emotional well-being, and of his spiritual growth.

It's impossible to overestimate the importance of the early months of life, both before and after birth. The quality of care we receive will contribute in every way to our health and well-being. As far as spiritual well-being is concerned, we should consider this early period as the time when the ability to trust develops. How can people ever truly trust in God if they haven't first learnt that it is safe to trust the significant people in their lives?

Strange though it will seem at the time, when we as parents are responding to our babies' needs – feeding, changing nappies, bathing, comforting, talking to them, playing with them, keeping them cool or warm, protecting them from danger – we are actually taking part in their spiritual development. We are teaching our child that the world is basically a good place – God's place. When unpleasant things happen — hunger pains, discomfort, loneliness, boredom, heat, fear — help and relief will come. The baby can grow up to be confident, knowing that people are to be trusted.

Those who learn that it is not safe to trust may grow up to be withdrawn, angry, depressed or over-timid. They may develop a closed-up attitude to life. But those who can trust will find it easier to be open to new possibilities, to people, to adventures of further trust and ultimately to the challenge of faith in God.

What really matters?

When Kath and Tom talk over how they will make sure that God is part of family experience for their child, they may decide on many kinds of observances — prayers at bedtime, for example — to make their experience of faith 'visible' in their home. They will choose what seems right to them and their choices will be changed and adapted as they learn what works for them in practice. (Prayers at bedtime may work well for one family but not prove to work for another family who feel happier saying prayers informally when out walking in the park or at mealtimes.)

What really matters, though, is not the outward signs, but what is happening between the child and his parents in the ordinary, everyday transactions of feeding, bathing and other kinds of care. Kath and Tom won't feel that they are doing anything special as they get up in the middle of the night to see to their fretful baby, or as they wake in the half-darkness of dawn to give an early feed. They may feel tired and grumpy. They will get bored of changing nappies and washing little garments. They will despair of ever having the chance to watch an entire television programme without being interrupted by their baby's demands, or to go out for an evening without feeling guilty or anxious.

Knowing that they are engaged in tasks that have sacramental importance to their child probably won't make them feel any better about the constant demands he makes on them. But what they *feel* isn't the issue. It's what they will be *doing for* and *being to* their child that has such enormous and far-reaching consequences.

In the most ordinary daily tasks, the most sacred work is done!

REFLECTION

If you love me, don't cling on to me as though
I was your possession. But don't let me go as
though I was not precious to you. Instead, hold
me in the palms of your hands like a newly-
hatched eagle on the face of the sheltering cliff.
Let me remain there as long as I need to, making
my blundering trial flights. Don't try to stop me
– I was born for flight. And when the time
comes for me to leave you, don't be anxious.
What you have taught me will keep the wind
under my wings.

4

The big event

They knew it was going to happen. They have been preparing for it for months and have hardly talked about anything else for the last few weeks. But when Tom and Kath hold their newborn son in their arms and gaze down into his tiny, puckered face, they find it hard to believe that it's true!

A sense of disbelief is quite common among parents, especially first-time parents. For some reason, it is almost impossible to accept that you have joined with God in an act of creation and produced between you a fully-formed person, another human being.

It is a miracle and, like other miracles, it takes time to adjust to what has taken place. Your family has grown. You are no longer just a couple. You are parents and have the awesome responsibility of caring for and providing for this small, vulnerable and infinitely precious person.

Tom and Kath experience joy, wonder and amazement at Warren's birth. There is also more than a little apprehension as they consider the commitment they have now undertaken.

Other reactions

The vast majority of new parents feel an overwhelming sense of happiness and relief, but this is not always the case. Sometimes, for no apparent reason, there can be a feeling of anti-climax. The mother or father may look at the child and think, 'Was it really worth it?' They may feel nothing at all; they may even feel resentful towards the baby. And a few days after the birth, most new mothers will feel depressed and tearful – a natural reaction to the exertions of the birth and the hormonal and physical changes their bodies are going through as they adjust to the post-natal needs of their baby.

These negative feelings can come as an unwelcome shock and may be very disturbing. It's very important to tell the medical staff about them. Feeling bad after your baby's birth, whether you are male or female, doesn't mean you're going to be a bad parent. If needed, special help is available, but this state is nearly always short-lived. It may be that you're overwhelmed with the demands being made on you – and the demands of adjusting to the birth, the baby and your new role are very great indeed. You may be just plain exhausted and only want to be left alone!

It is especially hard to be depressed when everyone is telling you how happy you must be. Talking about what you are experiencing is very helpful, though. Being an adequate parent doesn't depend on how you feel in the first few weeks of you baby's life, and nobody will think badly of you just because you aren't immediately filled with warm, parental love for your baby.

Other problems

The vast majority of new parents have healthy, thriving babies, but some have to face the news that their child is not well or has a physical or mental disability. A few babies even die or are born dead. In such cases, expert advice will be needed and expert care given to babies who are ill and to their parents.

It is hard to understand why newborn babies should be sick, suffer or die. Some people blame God. Others say that it proves he doesn't exist, for what sort of God would allow such things to happen? As Christians we won't necessarily have the answers to these problems, and anyone offering easy, slick answers wouldn't be giving genuine help or comfort to perplexed parents. Though we search the Bible to find out why these tragedies occur, we don't find neat solutions. We are left with our perplexity. In such cases, it is certainly not wrong to feel anger and grief and to express such feelings freely. Pretending to be calm or resigned won't help anyone cope with a difficult situation. I am sure that God doesn't expect us quietly to accept tragedy and trouble or to pretend it hasn't happened. Anger, grief and questioning are a necessary part of the process.

As Christians we do know that every baby that ever lives – however briefly, whether sick, healthy or disabled – is loved by God. He knows that, being human, we are all flawed in some way, yet he loves us with a passionate love. Imagine a nine-pound baby with a healthy appetite and a robust pair of lungs. In the same hospital there is a three-pound premature baby, lying half-alive in the incubator. Both are equal in God's love and regard. Both are unique, special and objects of his constant, loving goodwill.

The mystery of life remains a mystery. However, whatever happens, no human being is less of a human being than any other. No human being is less precious, less full of potential, less valuable to society than any other. Every birth is a cause for celebration.

Change all round

Now that Warren has arrived, Tom and Kath find at once that their relationship has changed in very significant ways. They can't simply go back to the way things used to be because they are beginning a new stage in their life together.

Being parents is a different way of life. Kath and Tom find that they no longer feel the same about themselves or about each other. The new feelings aren't necessarily negative, but they do have to be faced and talked about.

It may not be easy just now to find time to discuss the changes that are taking place, but a lot of misunderstanding can be avoided if couples are honest with each other. Little by little over the first few weeks they will re-negotiate their relationship to take account of the new state of affairs. It will be all too easy to allow issues like who does the shopping (Kath who is at home all day but is hampered by Warren and his erratic timetable, or Tom who would rather spend his time at home with Kath and the baby) to be decided with resentment and frustration on both sides. Discussing it openly turns the issue into a negotiation rather than a battle. In this, and in many other issues, Tom and Kath will have to try to remain in communication. It's no good pretending that they already know what the other is thinking.

Marking the occasion

The birth of every human being is a great occasion. The baby is not just part of the immediate family but belongs, in many ways, to the wider family, to the local community and to the religious community into which he is born. For these reasons, marking the baby's arrival in some way is usual in most societies.

Tom and Kath will have to decide before too long how

to celebrate Warren's birth. They could decide to keep it strictly private and simply offer a prayer of thanks as soon as they get home together. This would be right for some people in some situations, but most new parents want to hold a wider celebration.

It is a *family* occasion because, now that the baby has arrived, the shape of the family has been altered. Usually people welcome an opportunity for the family to meet together and welcome the new member.

It is a *community* occasion because the baby will already be making his presence felt in the neighbourhood. Just walk out with a pram and you will quickly discover how much interest a new baby causes, even from total strangers.

It is a *religious* occasion because most parents want to express their sense of thankfulness to God and to pray for their child. It is often a time, too, when new parents, especially mothers, become sensitive to the presence of God and to the spiritual side of life. This may be true even for those who have never felt like this before. Churches welcome those who come to mark the arrival of a baby.

It is important to get the occasion right, however. The new parents are the ones who must decide on what ought to happen. They shouldn't take part in a ceremony or ritual just to please others, though the expectations of their families may well be taken into consideration.

They may decide on a christening in church, but this isn't the only option. Many churches offer a service of thanksgiving and dedication. During the service, God is thanked for the baby, and the parents and church together promise to dedicate themselves to providing nurture and Christian example for the child. For others, a simple act of presenting the child to the church may be appropriate.

Whatever is chosen, it is important to note that no ceremony can make anything 'happen'. Ceremonies only mark what has happened or what is happening to people.

There is no 'magic' in any religious service to make God accept or love an infant more than he already does. Rituals are part of human life because they act as exclamation marks in our lives, times to look back upon and remember.

It will be important for Tom and Kath, for instance, to remember the welcome given to Warren by their families and by the church to which they belong. They will remember the promises made by the community and will wish to 'call in these promises' at various times during Warren's childhood. They will remember their own public promises more vividly than if they had made the same promises privately. And the occasion will give them assurance of God's love for them.

At a public occasion, if the couple wish, the changes in their relationship since the arrival of the baby can be acknowledged and prayed about by the church, family and community.

Above all, a ceremony is a statement that parents aren't alone. Bringing up a child *is* a great responsibility and the burden will almost certainly become too great for parents who try to do it without the advice, support and prayers of family, friends and community. This is something which has been lost in recent years, to the great disadvantage of children. Parents shouldn't have to struggle alone and children shouldn't be isolated from the influence and example of a wider community of caring people.

So, a ceremony in church with the family present can be a reminder to everyone of the way in which we all belong to each other, are responsible to each other and depend on each other.

How to please everyone?

A particular problem for Kath and Tom is that their families are not regular churchgoers, whereas for Tom and Kath church is very significant. Tom's parents, in particular, expect something much more formal than they are likely to get in Tom and Kath's church. For Tom's mother and father the outward paraphernalia – the way people dress, the things done to the baby, the photographs afterwards, the party and the cake – may be what really matters.

For Tom and Kath, these things are less important than the promises they make, the prayers that are said and the acknowledgement that Warren belongs to the church and is a child of God. Naturally enough, Kath feels irritated with her mother-in-law's interference and would cut family out altogether if she could. For her, the church is the proper point of reference for things to do with God, not the family, none of whom usually show much interest in spiritual matters.

A bit of diplomacy is needed here, for some vital issues are at stake! What would please God? This is what both Tom and Kath really want to discover – and they must do that in their own way. However, they would be wise to consider a few questions while they make their decision:

- How important a part in Warren's life will his grandparents play? Could the ceremony reflect the way in which parents and grandparents are going to work together and support each other?
- Is there some way of including the family in a special occasion, a way which will help them express what they feel about the new baby and which will be satisfying and comfortable for them?
- Should Kath and Tom go along with other people's arrangements just to keep the peace, or would irritation and resentment spoil the day anyway?
- Could there perhaps be *two* occasions, one for the family and one for the church community?
- When Warren gets older, how might he wish to have been welcomed?

REFLECTION

'[When Isaac was born,] Sarah said, "God has
brought me joy and laughter. Everyone who
hears about it will laugh with me." . . . The child
grew, and on the day that he was weaned,
Abraham gave a great feast.'
Genesis 21:5, 6, 8

'[Hannah said,] "I asked [the Lord] for this child,
and he gave me what I asked for. So I am
dedicating him to the Lord. As long as he lives,
he will belong to the Lord." '
1 Samuel 1:27–28

'The time came for Elizabeth to have her baby,
and she gave birth to a son. Her neighbours and
relatives heard how wonderfully good the Lord
had been to her, and they all rejoiced with her.'
Luke 1:57–58

5

Early days

Before Warren was born, Tom and Kath both thought that new parents made too much fuss about the amount of work babies are. They never said so, even to each other, but they secretly vowed not to let the baby interfere with their usual routine. Surely, it would only take a little organisation!

It hasn't taken Warren long to educate them both. Before he'd been home from hospital an hour, he became fretful. His parents tried everything to pacify him, but he just wouldn't settle. He woke them four times during the night, then slept solidly through the morning and Kath wouldn't let anyone wake him for the regular feed time that she had established during her stay in hospital. She was afraid that once he was awake he wouldn't go back to sleep again – and she felt so tired. He needed a lot of attention during the afternoon and on into the evening. That night, he slept a little better, only waking up three times.

It's not long before his parents are wondering what on earth they are doing wrong. They scarcely ever get a moment to themselves and even essential tasks like getting meals have to be fitted in somehow round Warren's demands.

The worst thing is not getting enough sleep. They feel that if only they could have one unbroken night's rest, they could get themselves organised, clear the backlog of work and settle down. But it never happens. When Warren sleeps at night, they lie half-awake, waiting for him to cry. When he is awake, they take turns trying to get him to settle again.

And so it goes on, week after week.

Whose fault is it?

For Tom, it's tempting to blame Kath. She's the mother and she ought to know what she's doing! She's always been a bit disorganised and now she can't even stick to a sensible routine. How he would love to walk out for an hour or two and leave her to it! When he gets home from work, he's tired and looking forward to some peace and quiet. Instead, he nearly always finds Kath angry or in tears and desperately overtired. Warren is usually crying or, if he's asleep, Kath will hardly let Tom speak in case his voice should waken the baby. Sometimes, they end up having a row. They both know it's stupid because it only makes matters worse, but feelings are running very high between them.

Yet Tom loves Kath and adores Warren. He is very proud of them both but when he's so tired, it's very hard to show it. And he isn't sure any more what role he's supposed to play in the family. It feels as though someone has changed the rules without telling him what the new ones are. He feels helpless.

For Kath, it's just as bewildering. She's doing all she can to be a good mother. She thinks of nothing but Warren and his needs, but somehow he never seems to be satisfied. Kath has never worked so hard in her life.

It's not all bad, of course. She enjoys being with her son and getting to know him. When she goes out with him or has a visitor, she is delighted to show the baby off and takes great pleasure in feeding him, talking to him and playing with him.

The trouble is that it's so tiring and the work is never-ending. Much of it is boring and provides no fulfilment at all and, because she is tied to Warren's unpredictable demands, she doesn't get out to meet other people as often as she would like to. Sometimes, she's so tired she doesn't want to see anyone anyway.

What's going on?

It's nobody's fault, of course. Every parent at this stage in a family's life will experience some of the following:

- exhaustion
- a feeling of helplessness
- fear of being not being able to cope
- boredom with routine tasks
- resentment at the loss of freedom
- loneliness
- panic

The same will happen every time there is a new baby in the family, not just the first time. More experienced parents, however, have usually learnt (whatever they feel about it) that it is impossible to be a perfect parent. Most parents start wanting to do all the right things in just the right way for their children. Being good parents – and being seen by others to be good parents – is very important to us. Sooner or later (usually sooner), we discover that we are not infinitely patient and wise. We keep failing. Most of us go on struggling against enormous odds with a huge sense of guilt.

Kath and Tom wanted to create a calm, peaceful atmosphere for their baby. They imagined him sleeping quietly while the housework was done. In their dreams, he would wake for leisurely feeds and be taken out for sunny rides to the shops or the park. They imagined quiet evenings alone or with friends while the baby was tucked up in his cot asleep.

That dream has died. They often seem to be battling against Warren. Tranquillity is precious but very rare. Kath is so angry at times because she can't quieten the baby that she shouts at him, and once she almost hit him. Tom sometimes pretends to be deeply asleep rather than get up in the middle of the night when Warren cries. Feeds are given in anger, nappies changed in temper, tears shed and many cross words said – by both of them. Kath and Tom have discovered that they are not really very good parents.

What can be done?

Perhaps the most helpful thing for new parents is to realise quickly that they aren't, and will never be, perfect parents. Only God is the perfect parent. The rest of us fail. What we can do, however, is to be reasonably good, responsible parents, who, by and large, do the best we can and are genuinely committed to our children.

The first step in being a responsible parent is to admit the need for help! This applies equally to couples and to lone parents. Talking about the problems may seem obvious, but it can be very hard to admit to other people that we're having a hard time. There is a strange myth in our society that parenting ought to come naturally, especially to women. We assume that people will just *know* what to do with their children and we receive very little education, except for our own experience of being parented.

How strange that this vital and complex job should be done without training or support! Yet millions of people do cope successfully with the challenge of being parents. In the past, though, bringing up children didn't take place in the hot-house of isolated homes but was a community task, shared by older generations and by friends and neighbours. This is still the case in some cultures, of course, and it provides a more biblical pattern of family life than the norm in our society (one or two parents taking on the entire responsibility for their children in isolation).

We need help. If we can't get it from our relations, who may live many miles away, it is even more important to find others who can share the burdens and the joys of raising children with us. We can build a wide network of support.

There may be other parents who live nearby in exactly the same situation. There may be older people around who would enjoy taking a grandparently role. As a community of God's family, the church is especially suited to meeting the needs of parents and children. Often parents get together informally within the church to share their experiences, arrange babysitting and support each other. Sometimes, there's an opportunity for parenting courses where people can talk openly about what is going on in their lives.

Whatever help is needed, it's better to look for it before reaching a crisis in the home. It's unlikely that any couple or single parent will make the adjustments needed when a baby arrives without some problem arising, so there's no shame attached to asking for help. It's our right. We don't need to manage alone.

Looking for solutions

For Warren's sake, Tom and Kath need to sort out what's going on in their relationship. They'll never achieve their dream of being a perfect couple with an ideal baby in a immaculate home. However, they can create an atmosphere in which Warren can thrive – one in which their marriage will also flourish.

They should admit to themselves and to each other those feelings listed earlier in this chapter. They'll need to promise each other to do so on a 'no blame' basis. It's not Kath's fault that she sometimes feels angry towards the baby, and Tom shouldn't blame her but try to understand the pressures that she's under. It's not his fault that he sometimes resents the way Warren takes all Kath's attention and saps her energy, leaving little for him. Kath must try to listen without getting angry at what he says. The idea isn't to blame each other for anything that's gone wrong but to see the other person's point of view.

The couple can do a lot to help each other – arranging and keeping regular times when each can have undisturbed time alone, for instance. This may relieve the pressure of the baby's constant demands.

They can look for help too – lots of it! There are excellent parenting books, courses (some of which are listed at the back of this book) and self-help groups. And there are friends, neighbours, church family, relatives who can reduce the pressures in all sorts of ways, depending on the needs of the parents. Whether parents feel more comfortable going to experts or just sharing with people they know, they'll benefit from opening out their family life. Just like taking the top off a bottle of fizzy drink, it takes away the pressure!

Yet, despite all the help in the world, Kath and Tom have to learn their own parenting style. They may listen to advice and to other people's experience of bringing up children, but in the end they have to work out what suits them and what suits Warren and any other children they may have – as we shall see in later chapters.

REFLECTION

God, our Father, you know that being a parent
means work, suffering and heartache as well as
fun, joy and pride. Help us to share both joy and
sorrow freely in our community so that we
enrich each other's lives and grow together as
your people, open to each other and to your love
– for the sake of our children and so that your
kingdom may come where we live.

6

Small world, isn't it?

One thing that often crosses the mind of a parent with a small baby is 'Is she doing it on purpose?' You sit down at last for a moment's peace, hoping to catch a few minutes of your favourite soap on TV, the football match or the novel you've been dying to read – and the baby starts to cry! She's slept peacefully while you coped with the mind-numbing, boring jobs; but just when you thought you would get a few moments to yourself, almost as though she knew what was going on, she has started to demand your attention.

If you're tired anyway, it's easy to feel that there's some malicious intent on your baby's part. Or maybe you think she's misbehaving – just playing up – when she won't settle at night. Or perhaps it occurs to you that it's because the baby is jealous that your cuddle or lovemaking with your partner is interrupted.

People often ask, 'Is she a good baby?' It usually means 'Is the baby much trouble?' but there is the implication that the baby is making moral choices about her behaviour and deciding whether to be good or bad. It suggests that she is able to understand her parents' situation and make a decision that will either please or displease them.

The baby's world

When Warren was born, his body was separated from his mother's and though the physical link is still maintained through feeding and by the care he is given, he is unaware of his own separate identity. He doesn't know where he ends and the rest of the world begins. As yet he hasn't had enough experience of the way the world is ordered to be able to distinguish between other people, other objects and himself. He will spend the first few months of his life working this out.

A routine and constant, reliable care will help him make this discovery. He will begin to recognise other people by their scent, by their voices and by sight. He will quickly learn that when he cries, one of his parents will come and comfort him. So, as he has no other means of getting what he wants, he will use what was once a crying response more purposefully.

He will learn two important things as a result of this which are, in fact, contradictory. The first is that he can summon help when he is in need – hungry, in pain, bored or uncomfortable. This will teach him that the world is a safe place, that he can trust it and that he is surrounded by loving care.

The second is that, sometimes, help will not come. Sooner or later, he will cry and nothing will happen for a while. Maybe he cries when Kath is taking a shower and Tom is making an important phone call. Both parents will know from the tone of the baby's voice that his need isn't urgent, so they will leave him to cry for a while until they are ready to deal with him. This kind of situation, provided it doesn't happen too often, will show Warren that he isn't all-powerful. He will discover that he cannot always have what he wants, just when he wants it. It is a valuable lesson in helping him to realise that other people have lives distinct from his own. He is not the centre of the universe.

This learning, though it is very important, must take place against the background of the consistent care he normally receives. There is no need for parents to plan for it to happen: it will, inevitably. And it will take a long, long time for a baby to gain a well–balanced self-image: he will be well into childhood, even beyond childhood. Indeed, this is something we work at throughout our lives, rather like maintaining a balancing act, sometimes thinking too little of ourselves and sometimes too much.

So, for Warren to be demanding isn't 'naughty' but normal and right for his age. When he wakes in the night feeling uncomfortable, he can't distance himself from his situation. He cannot possibly think, 'It's the middle of the night. I mustn't disturb anyone.' He operates in the only way he knows – he cries. He has no concept of his parents' need for sleep. He cannot imagine that they have any desire to do anything other than to come and meet his needs.

Learning about the world

As the months pass, Warren will begin to look more and more to the world around him. It's still a small world, consisting mainly of his home and the immediate area viewed from the safety of his pram or buggy. What he sees and hears will make little sense to him at first but will still be fascinating.

People will be of great interest to him, too. He will enjoy being spoken to, stroked, smiled at and played with. A baby's first smile, when he seems to recognise us and respond to us person–to–person is always an important milestone.

Play will begin quite early, too. Once Warren has

grasped the idea that his actions have consequences, he has a whole new world available to him. He can deliberately move his arms and legs, testing out how they work. He can reach out to touch and then grasp objects and bring them to his mouth. He can even play imaginary games, maybe turning away from the breast or bottle while he's feeding. He may whimper, pretending to cry before turning back to suckle.

If we're alert, we will notice these games and activities and allow time for them when possible. When we lift our baby out of the cot, we might notice that she's reaching out for the mobile above her head and give her a few minutes to play with it. We cannot be sure what the baby is learning from what she is doing, but if we make it a practice to allow time for play she will learn that her activities are of importance to us and will grow in self-confidence.

Children who are always interrupted when they're at play are being taught not to value their own activities very highly and won't be able to give their full concentration to what they are doing. So parents should make necessary demands upon children in a courteous way, waiting for the right moment to interrupt rather than demanding instant attention. Later on, we can give advance warning of what is going to happen, eg 'We'll be going out in a few minutes.'

This doesn't mean that parents can never interrupt play. That would be foolish and very inconvenient for the whole family. It's a matter of establishing normal practice in the home – that even a baby can have the opportunity to finish a task she has begun or a game she is playing. It's a matter of courtesy, presumably one of the things parents want to teach their children.

Give and take

From her very earliest days, a baby will communicate with people around her. Human beings have the greatest range of communication skills of any species and all these skills are learnt.

A mother was once asked, 'Why don't you ever speak to your baby?'

She replied, 'Because he never talks to me.'

How sad! The fact is parents have to take the initiative. We are the ones who will teach our children to communicate and the more we put into it, the more our children will respond.

Some parents, probably unwittingly, demonstrate means of communicating that are less effective, like shouting to get our own way, bullying or giving people 'the cold shoulder'. Others teach really useful skills like the art of mediating when there's a difficulty, how to show love through touch, how to maintain a friendly silence, how to listen, how to encourage others.

Even the way a parent handles a baby is a means of communication. From the first a newborn baby is able to respond, picking up whether the parent is anxious or relaxed. For this reason, relaxed parents tend to have relaxed babies and anxious parents have anxious babies, which hardly seems fair to first-time parents still trying to come to terms with their new role!

Talking to a baby isn't just about teaching him words he will eventually say. Talking engages the baby's attention, sometimes for fairly lengthy periods. Most people seem to know what to say to babies, though some don't want to be overheard!

There's no need for 'baby talk' as the baby doesn't understand 'beddybies' any more easily than 'bed'! And, though it is instinctive to speak more slowly to an infant, it is better not to adopt a special 'baby' tone of voice,

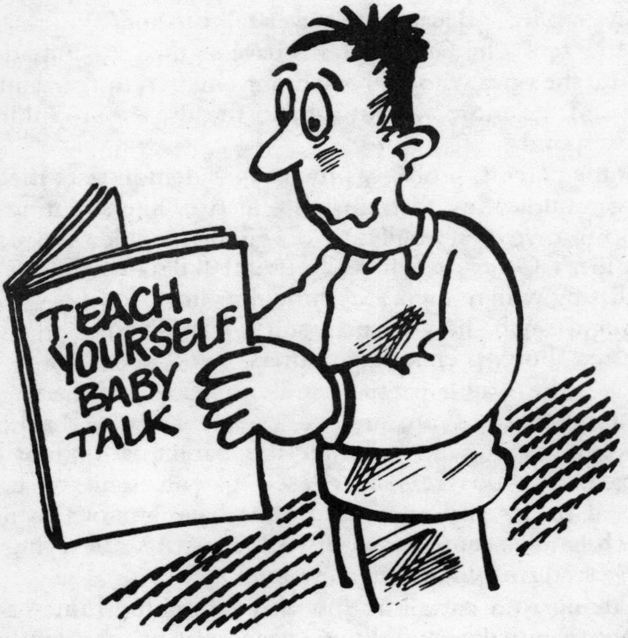
TEACH YOURSELF BABY TALK

since at some stage this will have to be dropped. Talking to an older child in a 'baby' way causes embarrassment to all concerned!

It is interesting to watch a parent talking to a baby. You might imagine that it would be fairly one-sided, but not so. The baby, only a few weeks old, begins to move her arms and legs to the music of the speech, reacting with her whole body. At a few months old, she is talking back, making her own burbled comments of delight. Soon she learns to take turns, listening for a while, then making her own noises in reply. She is learning the give-and-take of communication, even though she may not yet know that the noises you make can have meaning. She certainly cannot express any meaning herself verbally, though her sounds will become more and more expressive.

This stage is a bit like the early stages of learning to read. You first have to understand that books contain meaning and that the meaning is conveyed in the printed shapes on the page. You have to realise that you can decode the words and you have to want to do it. You will then learn to read left to right, top to bottom of the page. The process becomes more precise and technical, but the first stages are most important. You will never learn to read if you never see anyone else reading a book.

So, to learn to speak, you need someone to share the pleasure of conversation with you. Parents who talk and talk and talk to their children do them a great service (as long as they do an equal amount of listening). Not only are they giving them a head-start in education, but they are affirming that their children are valuable to them. The baby who is allowed time for 'talking' to her mother is receiving a message about the value of her contribution. That child is being prepared to know her value to God and to understand that she can both receive from and give to him.

Working for the long term

Through the early months a relationship is developing between the parent and child. The ability to make a relationship is fundamental to a child's healthy life-style and vital to spiritual growth.

The hours Tom and Kath spend with Warren are of enormous significance to him. When they begin to understand all that they are giving to him, they will be able to bear the difficulties of this period more easily. The problem is that there is no short-term result of their day-to-day care. It all seems rather mundane at the time. One thing is certain, though. Sooner or later, parents will reap what they have sown during their child's infancy. It's worth putting in a lot of work, love and prayer at this stage!

REFLECTION

I felt that I shouldn't spend time cooing over my baby. There was so much else to do when he was small. So I got on with the work and tried to teach him to be more independent. Of course, I gave him lots of toys to play with so he wouldn't be bored, and hung mobiles above his cot to occupy him. He learnt not to demand attention in the end. Now he's a man and I'm old, I regret it all. He rarely comes to see me and when he does, he seems so hard and cold. Almost as though he has no love inside him.

What could be the long-term effects of failing to give children much attention? What are the effects of giving lots of attention?

7

On the move

Warren is on the move, and suddenly the house has to be reorganised! Books and papers are no longer scattered on the furniture or on low shelves. Precious ornaments are moved to higher and higher ledges around the house. A lock has been fixed to the fridge. The playpen, in which Tom and Kath had hoped Warren would spend many happy hours, has instead become the resting place of the sewing machine, the banjo and other things that his parents don't want Warren to get at.

The baby is into everything and there's no stopping him. As soon as something attracts his attention, he must have it. Both Tom and Kath spend much of their time chasing after him as he crawls at express speed towards the shiny baubles on the Christmas tree or a visitor's carelessly abandoned bag.

It won't be long, of course, before Warren is walking and his range and speed is increased enormously, yet he is still totally unaware of the dangers around him. As he grabs hold of the attractive bleach bottle, he is dismayed when Kath snatches it away and shouts at him. No wonder he yells and cries! It seems so unfair.

Physical boundaries

Any parents who failed to surround their children with safe physical boundaries would be regarded as negligent. Gates, fireguards, bolts, locks, harnesses and reins – all could be regarded as restricting a child's freedom, but we all know that they are there for her safety. Parents want to provide a safe environment in which their children can live and play freely without any danger of coming to harm. The boundaries define the safe area and no parent would dream of opening the garden gate on to the busy road because their child wanted to play in the street.

Usually, soon after the child begins to stand up and explore the physical world, she will discover that she can influence events. A wonderful, magical word comes into her vocabulary – 'No!' The child might hear this word a lot as her parents try to stop her damaging herself and the home in her first explorations. But at some point every child will realise the possibilities of *saying* no. It's an important stage in a child's life. It means that she is reaching for independence, realising that she's an individual with the right to express what she wants for herself. It's a landmark in the process of growing up.

Yet it comes as a shock to Tom and Kath when Warren begins to refuse to do things that he had done quite happily before. Suddenly – no, he's not going to have his shoes put on. No, he won't sit on Kath's lap while she brushes his hair. No, he won't be fed the last spoonfuls of his breakfast – he wants to do it himself, however long it takes.

What surprises them is the strength of his protests. Even the smallest conflict turns into a real power battle. Their (on the whole) contented and compliant baby has become a monster almost overnight.

Coping with conflict

Understanding what has happened can ease the anxiety of this period considerably. To Kath and Tom it feels as though Warren has become their enemy. In fact he needs their love and gentleness as much as ever. It's just as frightening and confusing for him!

Warren must learn to be independent. He isn't going to be a child forever. In a few years he will be expected to make important decisions on his own and ultimately he has to deal with all the complexities of adult life. Of course, he doesn't know this yet but something inside him is urging him to get started. It's a process that began when he was born, and now that he is more aware of himself as an individual, he has to explore just what it means.

At first his experiments with independence are very crude and not at all rational. He doesn't know why his mum and dad are making him go shopping when he wants to have a picnic in the park like he did yesterday. His parents' explanations (that it's raining and anyway they have to go shopping) are of no use to him. The promise of a picnic another day doesn't interest him. He wants to have a picnic now! He feels that he has a right to have what he wants and he is angry at being denied it. So he begins to cry and shout and refuses to put on his shoes to go shopping.

He has a long way to go in terms of learning what is reasonable. He doesn't know the limit of his parents' power (eg to stop the rain if they wanted to). Nor does he understand that they cannot do just what *they* want to do (eg that they have to go shopping even when they don't want to or there will be nothing to eat). He only knows that he isn't getting what he wants and he is trying out strategies to reverse this state of affairs. In his totally self-centred world this seems the right thing to do, but at the same time it scares him to incur the displeasure of the very people he loves and needs so much.

A toddler is still at the very beginning of learning what is right and wrong. Only through trial and error can he begin to discover what right and wrong mean. So, when Warren screams and stamps his feet in temper, he isn't necessarily being 'naughty', turning into a rebel or trying to overthrow his parents.

What he is saying is something like this (though he can't express it in words): 'I am finding out that I can have my own views about the way things are run, but I don't know yet how to handle that power.' Saying no, refusing to cooperate, shouting and crying are Warren's first attempts to make his influence felt.

What his parents have to do is gently and firmly to show him good, appropriate ways of expressing his own individuality. At the same time they will, just as gently and firmly, discourage tantrums by showing Warren that he won't get what he wants that way.

Safe boundaries

Believe it or not, a toddler having a tantrum is scared. She wants and needs the security that her parents have provided but the drive for independence urges her to test the boundaries all the time. The worst thing at this stage is for a child to discover that there are no boundaries, that she only has to push and the safe, secure walls crumble away. It is most important that her parents don't give in to her demands all the time. On the other hand, it is vital that they do give her more and more opportunities to express preferences and to make choices *within the safety of known boundaries*.

So, for instance, it would be stupid for Tom to give in to Warren's refusal to hold his hand while crossing the road. Tom must win that battle, of course, though it need not be resolved by a big show of power on Tom's part.

Perhaps he might give Warren a choice of *where* to cross the road or which hand to hold, or distract Warren's attention by pointing at a passing ambulance before taking his hand and crossing.

If Warren refuses to get into the buggy to go shopping, he might be allowed to walk 'as far as the end of the road' or to choose which of two jackets to wear to keep him warm or to be asked which shop, the supermarket or the newsagent, he would like to go in first. Kath will know that Warren can't walk all the way to the shops yet, but she will be wise to distract him from the immediate conflict and not make it a point of honour that she must win and be seen to win. Eventually, if she is firm and persistent, she will have Warren in the buggy and have avoided a major show-down.

If Tom and Kath can stand back and reflect on these incidents, they will realise how dreadful it would be if Warren were never to want to cross the road on his own or get out of the buggy and walk. Nobody wants to have teenagers who still need that level of care! Warren isn't asking for anything wrong. It's just that his timing is a little premature. As yet he has no idea of how much he has to learn before, for instance, he can cross the road on his own. He cannot have all he asks for just yet, but it is a good thing that he wants to be self-reliant. It's a sign that he is reaching out for independence, which is something, surely, that all parents want for their children.

Full independence is a long way off for Warren and he will need both his parents for many years to come. In the meantime, their job is to protect and restrain him in areas in which he is not yet responsible, while allowing him to exercise more responsibility as he becomes able to do so.

A two year-old, for instance, can choose between two items to be cooked for his tea (but not answer the question 'What would you like for tea?' which offers too many options and may end in conflict if he asks for something which isn't available or just silly), or whether to wear his green or blue jumper (but not to decide on his entire outfit, since he cannot take proper account of the weather or the activities he will be doing during the day).

Dignity

Apart from maintaining safe boundaries, parents with toddlers at this stage need to be careful to protect the dignity and self-esteem of their children. Humiliating children into submission is as harmful as giving in to them. It is vital to their spiritual growth that they gain a healthy self-image and this can only be done by children whose experience of life teaches them that they are valued and valuable. If we as parents can both set boundaries and encourage increasing independence, we are helping to promote our child's spiritual growth.

The child shouldn't be too restricted, nor be too 'free'. Too much restriction crushes his self-esteem and gives him a negative view of himself as always in the wrong, perhaps 'naughty' and deserving of rejection. Too much freedom, on the other hand, gives a child more power than she can handle and presents frightening choices which, far from spelling freedom, bring fear and may actually inhibit the growth of responsibility.

A loving parent demands obedience in such a way that the child is affirmed and encouraged. If the parent tries to break the child's will, serious damage can be done to her spiritual and emotional well-being. The relationship between parent and child will also be damaged. This will hinder the child as she grows in faith, because the image of a parent who humiliates and forces obedience will always project itself onto her growing understanding of God the Father.

Yet the Bible's picture of God is not of one who forces us to obey against our will. He is a God who delights in loving, glad obedience. Angry, resentful obedience damages our relationship with him. He wants to be obeyed by those who trust him, not by those who fear his displeasure. He is a God who preserves our dignity, as we can clearly see when we look at stories of how Jesus dealt with people. This is the basis of a Christian's relationship with God. Christian parents have the privilege of introducing their children to God as they try to model his love and consistent care to their children.

We have the awesome responsibility and privilege of being our children's first 'pictures of Christ', just as Jesus is our picture of God. That means that what they know about God and about Jesus, they learn from what they see in us, by the way we treat them and others and the example of love that we set.

We fall short – that goes without saying! But when we fail we know that, just as we forgive our children when they fail, so God forgives our failure. There's always the opportunity of another chance with him!

REFLECTION

'Children, . . . obey your parents, for this is the right thing to do . . . Parents, do no treat your children in such a way as to make them angry. Instead, bring them up with Christian discipline and instruction.'
Ephesians 6:1, 4

How can parents make it easy for their children to obey them?

8

No two are the same

Tom and Kath have always been proud of Warren, just as we are all proud of our children. Naturally, they both want him to do well and grow up to be someone special. There's nothing wrong with parents having ambitions so long as those ambitions don't become prisons for their children.

It was with some pleasure that Warren's parents (and the rest of the family) watched his progress over the first few months. Kath was proud to be able to tell her mother that Warren seemed quick to learn. He was first among the babies of similar age in Kath's circle of friends to sit up by himself and the first to crawl. On the day that he first walked, Tom couldn't wait to ring up his parents and tell them about it!

Recently, though, they haven't been quite so happy. Warren is two and so is Simran, their neighbour's child. Simran is able to talk quite well and is even managing to string simple sentences together, but Warren seems to be stuck at single words. He says, 'Mum', 'Dad', 'dog', 'apple' and, of course, 'no' but never goes any further than that.

This seems unfair to Tom and Kath because they have

spent so much time talking to him, listening to his baby-sounds, reading to him, pointing things out to him, saying nursery rhymes, singing – all the right things to help him. When they hear Simran talking to Gita, her mum, and having such fun with language, it makes them realise how undeveloped Warren's speech is. It's hard for them to accept that Warren is backward.

They all get there in the end!

Or is he? As parents, we often compare our children with others of the same age, but it really is a wrong thing to do. Sometimes, of course, when some stage of development has been delayed for too long, we should be concerned. An inability to speak might be caused by deafness, for instance, and, if there is anxiety about this, then a GP or health worker will be able to help. On the other hand, slowness to learn to speak might just mean a temporary interest in something else which is more important to the child at that moment. One day, provided she is surrounded by speech in many forms, she will feel the need to express herself in words and may learn to talk very quickly.

I knew a boy whose first recorded words were, 'Don't turn off the telly. I'm watching it.' His family were astonished! He was about three years old and had never said more than single words before (and very rarely too). It's obvious, though, that this child *had* been learning to talk but had kept his learning to himself until he was ready to show it. He wasn't backward at all, though his family had been very anxious about him. He just needed time.

I also knew a girl who didn't learn to crawl until she was over a year old. Then, very suddenly and very steadily, she began to walk three months later, and never overbalanced or even stumbled. During those three months she had passed rapidly through all the stages from first crawling to independent walking. Children who begin earlier may take longer to gain the skill and balance needed to walk steadily.

I am sure that there are thousands of such stories. They all go to prove that, by and large, the vast majority of children gain the skills they need to live a normal adult life. Yet they don't all do things at the same ages. Some will take a faster, some a slower pace. Some who begin quickly may never achieve what others, who were slower, will achieve.

There's no point in comparing children with each other in terms of being forward or backward. I suppose it's inevitable that parents will do this, but the age at which a child cuts her first tooth, for instance, tell us nothing about her worth as a person! Such matters are merely interesting, not significant in terms of cleverness or ability.

It takes all sorts!

Kath has decided not to return to work until Warren starts school. At first she thought she would miss the people at work, but she has discovered that having a small child is a perfect opportunity to make new friends. She enjoys visiting and being visited by lots of parents and their children, and this makes her aware of how many different kinds of parents and children there are!

In fact, the phrases 'an average child' and 'a normal parent' don't have any meaning at all. Everybody has their own way of doing things and their own problems.

Tidiness

Some parents are obsessively tidy and organised. They get very upset when their children are messy and apologise to visitors for the toys and biscuit crumbs on the floor and furniture. Warren makes his home untidy too, but it doesn't worry Kath. To her it's more important that Warren can move around freely and play with a wide variety of toys in the way he likes. She finds it irritating and upsetting to see other parents scolding their children for making a mess, and thinks this is damaging. She notices that fussy parents have children who are more fretful and demanding than those whose parents don't worry so much about tidiness and cleanliness. Her way of coping with the problem is to tidy up the toys only once a day when Warren is in bed, no matter who is coming round. Visitors just have to be careful where they walk and sit! Cleaning gets done often enough, but Kath has got used to the windows being covered in smeary marks all the time. It's just the way things are until Warren grows up!

Meal times

In some homes Kath finds that meal times have a certain structure. Everyone sits around the table and remains there until the meal is over. Sometimes the children are given their meals at different times to adults. In other homes things happen more haphazardly. Children are fed when they say they're hungry and get a series of snacks; or when a meal is prepared, they're handed the food to eat where they please.

Kath and Tom made a conscious decision to try to eat together as a family whenever they could. They feel that meals are more than just times to eat but are occasions to meet together and share even when, at times, there is nothing much to say. There is more going on than consuming food. Meal times together strengthen the family sense of belonging. Kath and Tom see the time spent around the table as valuable, not only for Warren, but for themselves as a time of meeting in a busy world, a time when every individual is important and has the opportunity to give to and receive from other people. What is being shared? There are many things – love, care, personal attention, laughter, conversation, questions and answers, to name but a few. Of course, there can be other times in the day when this kind of sharing happens, but meal times occur regularly and don't need anybody to take a special initiative to make them happen. Unlike bed time, bath time, story time and other special times of sharing that small children enjoy, meals don't stop when children get older. The sharing can go on whenever people get together at whatever stage the family is at.

As Christians, it is significant to Kath and Tom that Jesus told his disciples to remember him when they ate and drank.

Difficult children

One of the things that has struck both Kath and Tom as Warren grows up is that almost everyone has a difficult child! Nobody is having an easy, problem-free time. Most parents are anxious about *some* aspect of their children's behaviour.

A mother with an aggressive child may envy her friend whose child is quiet. Yet her friend may be anxious that her child doesn't seem able to stand up for himself. It's embarrassing for Kath when Warren snatches toys from smaller children and hits out at them when they resist him. It's just as embarrassing for Gita when Simran refuses to kiss her grandparents and cries when anyone but Gita picks her up. They both feel as though their child's behaviour reflects badly on them, as though other people must be thinking what bad parents they are. The same is true of parents whose children have tantrums in the supermarket, kick strangers or throw food about at parties. We all want our children to behave well, especially in public, because we don't want to be shown up.

This is a totally unrealistic expectation and it is a shame

that our society has only disapproval for parents who are trying to deal with their children in public.

On a crowded commuter train a little girl suddenly realised that she had forgotten to bring a particular book to amuse herself with. An adult in the same position would have thought, 'Bother, I wish I'd remembered to bring that book.' But for the child it was a disaster. She wasn't open to reason. Her mother tried to point out that it didn't matter much as she had another book and anyway they were nearly at their destination. (In fact the scene went on for a good ten minutes which can seem like a very long time to a child. I bet it did to the mother too!) All the time the child got more and more worked up. She started to blame her mother and the mother replied that it was totally the child's fault. Then the mother began to threaten the child with what would happen if she didn't stop crying and making a fuss. The result of this was that the child got more worked up than ever.

The other passengers were able to hear every word. It must have been an ordeal for the mother, especially as several of them sighed loudly or clicked their tongues because their peace was being shattered.

The child's point of view

A very small percentage of human behaviour is inborn. Compared to reptiles, which emerge from the egg as miniature adults, we have to learn almost all we need to know. We do have inborn tendencies and personalities, but we need to learn to deal with our 'raw material' as we grow up. Because we are all individuals, that learning will take different forms for all of us. Take, for example, the little girl on the train. She was in the process of learning a great deal:

- How to handle her anger at forgetting something

- About the constraints of time and space (she couldn't make her mother go home; it would take too long)
- The behaviour that is acceptable in a crowded train
- Having sometimes to accept second-best
- How readily or otherwise her mother would give in to her

The parent's point of view

The mother was learning too. She was trying out a range of different strategies to stop her daughter's difficult behaviour – reasoning, threatening, blaming. The fact was that none of these worked because they weren't appropriate to the situation.

Reasoning didn't work because the child was very upset and felt unreasonable.

Threatening didn't work because the child wasn't concerned with what might happen in the future, only with what was happening at the moment. (Incidentally, the mother threatened to get off at the next station and leave the child alone. This frightened the little girl and actually made her more hysterical. It is wise not to use threats that we don't intend to carry out.)

Blaming didn't work because the child was so angry and upset that she couldn't see that forgetting the book was her own fault. Even if she had been able to accept the blame, it wouldn't have helped her feel any better about the situation.

Perhaps *distraction* might have worked. If the mother had got her daughter to think about something else, she might have been able to calm her down. The trouble was that they were both so worked up that neither of them could think clearly!

What does the child need?

Children need our help not our anger, blame or contempt, as they take their first steps in learning how to deal with themselves in a very complex society. It is important to note here that parents shouldn't necessarily see their children's behaviour as a reflection on themselves. Having a child who bites babies doesn't make us a bad mother or father. Many parents find their children doing things that seem outrageous! The question is how we can help our children learn to deal with the impulses that produce socially unacceptable behaviour.

We need to find responsible ways of helping children to cope with problems as they arise, ways that are not only effective, but that enable them to grow in self-esteem. This will be looked at in the next chapter.

REFLECTION

I am human. I'm an individual. I'm unique, not
a carbon copy of anyone else. I must find my
own way and make my own mistakes. It's a
dangerous journey but one I must go on. I am
not alone. You are on your own dangerous
journey beside me.

So, as we travel together, please share your
wisdom with me and I will share my innocence
with you. You will teach me how to grow up
loved and accepted by others, how to take
responsibilities, how to earn respect, how to be
an adult.

And I will teach you how to wonder at the
raindrops, how to splash in puddles, how to sing
when you're happy and cry when you're hurt,
how to be a child – become like a child again,
how to know God who loves children.

9

Moulding the clay

It was on his second birthday that Tom realised Warren was no longer a baby. Perhaps it was the new clothes that he was wearing that suddenly made him look more grown up. Tom had a feeling that a new era was dawning, an era in which he was going to be more and more important to his son.

Between the ages of two and five astonishing changes take place. The child learns how to master language and how to control and use her body so that she becomes more and more independent of adults. A two year-old will need lots of help with getting dressed and feeding herself, for instance, but a five year-old will be able to manage nearly everything herself. A two year-old, even when surrounded by other children, will still relate mainly to her parents, but a five year-old will probably set off confidently to play with friends, giving her parents hardly a backward glance.

Growing independence

Tom and Kath have noticed a difference between Warren's level of independence and that of Simran, Gita's daughter – and it is one that they are pleased about! Warren is friendly and doesn't mind who comes to his home. He is happy to be left with any of a number of friends and relatives. As a result, Kath and Tom can go out regularly together.

Gita's situation is different. Simran becomes distressed if she is left with anyone else, even her own grandparents or any of her other relatives. She follows Gita everywhere and seems to be constantly anxious that her mother will disappear if she lets her out of her sight. Gita can't go out much without Simran because it is too upsetting to leave her daughter screaming and having to be restrained in someone else's arms. Gita's mother says Gita shouldn't worry about leaving Simran in distress so that she learns to do without Gita. This puts Gita under pressure to do something that seems wrong to her. Causing Simran unhappiness doesn't seem a very good way of helping her be more independent.

What does Simran need to learn? Once Gita has worked that out, she can decide how to tackle the problem and she can enlist her mother's help so that they aren't always fighting over it.

Perhaps Simran is developing a very deep and complex relationship with her mother. She intuitively understands her mother's moods. She watches how her mother relates to other people and is learning how she deals with lots of different people in a sensitive and caring way. She is listening to the way her mother speaks and feels comfortable with her ways of doing things. Later, when she is older, she will model her own relationships, habits and use of language on her mother's. The time spent with her mother is vital to Simran because she is unconsciously learning to see the world as her mother sees it before she goes out to make it her own.

If this is so — and it may be — when Gita isn't there, Simran loses the structure of her world. She is 'all at sea' because there are no landmarks.

It is different for Warren. He actively enjoys new experiences. He likes to taste 'the fruit from lots of trees' and he is constructing his view of the world in this way. Of course, Tom and Kath are a very major influence in Warren's life, but he likes variety. He thrives on breadth.

Simran prefers depth — and there is nothing wrong with that! It is trying and worrying for Gita at the moment because it looks as though Simran will never be independent. She fears that Simran's clinginess shows weakness of character, and finds it hard to resist her mother's insistence to be 'harder' on Simran.

Actually, both Warren and Simran have the same basic need — to feel safe. Watch Warren and children like him. As soon as he feels threatened, you'll see that he wants Mum or Dad too!

Simran will branch out but only when she feels safe. This is unlikely to happen, however, when people are always threatening to take away the person with whom she feels most secure. Gita's instinct is probably right — to allow Simran to stay with her as much as possible. At the same time, of course, she will introduce her to different people and take her to many different places, but she will let Simran take things at her own pace. If she goes to a party, she should be allowed to view the proceedings from the safety of her mother's lap and not made to feel that she is a party pooper. If she goes to a fun fair, she may prefer to watch others on the rides.

Gita can be sure that one day Simran will feel confident enough to leave her. That day will be sooner, rather than later, if Simran is allowed to take her own initiatives when she feels ready. Trying to force a child to be independent

ruins her confidence. It is far better to leave her to trust her own judgment about what is safe. Then, on the day she finally leaves home, you will know she is on a far better footing than someone who has always been made to rely on someone else's judgment.

There will be problems of another kind with Warren, of course! He also needs to learn what is safe and what isn't. He will have to discover when to restrain his impulse to trust everything and everyone that comes his way. It is a dangerous world and he will have to be taught the boundaries of safety.

The issue of discipline

Discipline has very little to do with anger, shouting and punishment. Here's a picture to illustrate what I mean.

Two teachers take a class of children on a school trip. To get to the nature reserve that they are going to explore, they have to cross some marshy land. To make this as safe as possible, boards have been laid across the marsh so that the class can cross without getting their feet wet. The first teacher takes half the class first. She says, 'Don't you dare put one foot on the marsh. I warn you, if any of you stray off the boards, you'll be in big trouble. Just stay on the path and don't even think about going in the mud.' The chances are that at least one child will prefer the allure of the mud to the dull walk across the boards.

The other teacher says, 'I want you all to know what marsh land is like. Who wants to test this ground out? Put these wellies on and press your foot down gently. Do you see how quickly you begin to sink? When we get back, you can all have a go at doing that, but first we have to get safely to the nature reserve. Can anyone tell me how the wardens have solved the problem of getting us to the reserve without us all sinking into the marsh? As we walk along the boards, I want you to look out for the plants on the sheet I've given you. See if you can tell me later just where each one was growing.'

One group has been disciplined — the second group. They have been told about the dangers of the marsh, which will help them make wise decisions about keeping safe as they cross to the nature reserve. They have also been given something else to focus on — a task which is linked with the purpose of the visit. They have been given an opportunity to satisfy their curiosity about the marsh too. (Much so-called 'naughtiness' springs from children's natural and proper curiosity. They do need to find out about things. Discipline involves setting acceptable boundaries for curiosity, not curbing it altogether.)

So with our children, we shouldn't view discipline as a means of forcing them to do what we want. This is bullying, not discipline. Instead, discipline is about the following.

Giving information so that children make good decisions. There may be occasions when you cannot explain why they must do certain things, but it's better in the long run to train them to listen to your reasons. You may have to 'pull rank' from time to time because children are only just learning to reason and logic isn't always their strong point. 'I'm sorry, you can't have your own way this time' is still your right while they are small.

Focusing on positive behaviour. Many parents give their children lists of things they can't do but never tell them what they *can* do. If we keep talking about things that are forbidden, it shouldn't be a surprise that our children are always thinking about them! It's much easier to keep them off the dangerously high slide in the playground if we tell them that they *can* go on the swings or the round-about or the climbing frame.

Rewarding good, acceptable behaviour. One mistake that parents sometimes make is to give children the reward of our attention only when they are misbehaving. Wise parents praise their children when they are doing good, acceptable things: when they're playing constructively, keeping the rules of the home or trying to do something new (even if they don't succeed). They talk to their children about having to go shopping and what they are going to buy and involve them in making straightforward choices about items on the supermarket shelves. They point out how the checkout tills work and encourage the children to pick out all the cans from the shopping to pack. They encourage their children to tell them what they can see on the way home. Children are greedy for attention. Is it any wonder, then, that children who only get attention when they are misbehaving decide to lie on the ground and yell?

Encouraging self-discipline. Our ultimate aim is for our children to have the ability to be responsible for themselves. While they're small, parents and others who care for children have to think for them to a very large degree. They haven't yet enough knowledge or reasoning ability to be able to have too much freedom. But we can lay the foundations.

First, we can offer an example of being self-disciplined. I must say here that there's no parent in the world who will be able to offer a perfect example to his or her children, so don't worry if, from time to time, you fail. On the other hand, children won't learn to be self-disciplined if their parents have no moral standards. The same applies if parents consistently fail to put into practice what they teach their children. They cannot give in to every little whim they have and then expect their children to be self-restrained. This aspect of discipline is *the power of example.*

Second, we can sometimes allow children to suffer from the consequences of their own actions. It's not always sensible to do this, for instance if the child's health, sense of security or physical safety are at risk. On the other hand, we shouldn't always 'make things right' for them. There are times when it's right for them to learn that there are consequences to being careless, to hitting others, to being rude, to breaking or losing things, to refusing to eat or drink. These can be direct consequences, eg if you break a toy, you can no longer play with it. Or it might be something which you, as a parent, do to make the point, eg 'I will not let you hit people, so I want you to sit beside me until you have decided to play in a friendly way'. Parents have to be firm. We could call this aspect of discipline *experiencing justice*.

Third, we should always bear in mind that children are learners. It is natural for them to experiment with different types of behaviour and to see what works for them and what doesn't. Just because some children tell lies, it doesn't follow that they will turn into dishonest adults. It does mean, though, that they need to learn that lying isn't a good thing. It has certain unpleasant consequences and honesty, in fact, pays a better dividend in the long run.

So, when we become aware that our children are telling lies, we don't need to come down very hard on them immediately. They are learners and this is a good learning situation. We want them to know it is wrong, of course, but most of all we want to help them learn why it is wrong and what they can do instead when they're in a situation where honesty is difficult. We must remember how young and inexperienced they are and put ourselves at their disposal to help them learn to cope in the best way.

The same applies to a child having a tantrum. This can be shocking and embarrassing, as everyone with a toddler knows. Our response is very important. Difficult though it is, especially if the tantrum happens in a public place, we need to keep calm and bear in mind that we want the child to learn that this kind of behaviour just won't work. There's no need for us to panic or feel guilty about it. We can just wait until it's over, then comfort her and help restore her dignity. It is a hard lesson to learn that you can't always have your own way and it is best learnt in an atmosphere of support. We should never make the lesson harder by humiliating the child. Nor should we confuse the child by giving in for the sake of peace and quiet. Parents have to be understanding and flexible. We could call this aspect of discipline *compassion*.

Discipline and spiritual growth

Example, justice and compassion — these are all familiar to believers as pictures of the way God relates to us. All three are present in the biblical picture of God and of his Son, Jesus. As we strive to be an example to our children, as we show them justice and compassion, we're giving them a picture of God which will remain with them all their lives.

Conversely, if parents are self-indulgent or neglectful, or if they are too harsh or too lax, their children will find it harder as they grow up to relate to God as he really is.

But once again it needs to be said that if parents make the occasional, small slip (or even the occasional, large slip), God is compassionate on them too! He knows we fail as parents and he always gives us another chance. We shouldn't expect to be perfect parents. We cannot even expect to be 'good' parents, not all the time anyway. The struggle to be 'good' parents is too much for most of us and can lead to disillusionment about our task. On the other hand, we can all strive to be 'good enough' for our children. Basically, this means being committed to our children's welfare and finding our way step by step —

learning on the job. We aren't trying to be experts who know all the answers, but should see ourselves in partnership (not in competition) with our children.

Working in partnership with our children might mean the following:

- We do everything to build up their self-esteem by treating them as equal to ourselves.
- We help them overcome problems that arise with their behaviour, remembering that we too have our faults.
- We enlist their co-operation whenever possible and avoid ordering them about.
- We never humiliate them but always treat them with respect. We expect them to treat us with respect in return.
- We treat being with them and listening to them as a priority. We take their talk and activities seriously.
- If we let them down, we admit it to them and do all we can to put things right.

The idea of partnership doesn't end with our relationship with our children. Parenting is a tough task and we need others who will help us. Thankfully, we can include God himself, the perfect companion, helper and partner.

REFLECTION

You know, Father God, sometimes I have really good days. The kids behave and we have fun together – you know, go out for a walk or kick a ball about in the park. At the end of the day, when they're fast asleep in bed, I think, 'Well, I'm not doing such a bad job. They're good kids and I wouldn't change them for the world.'

On other days, it's no fun at all. The kids are a pain. They seem to have decided to spoil everything I try to do and I end up screaming at them. That's when I think I've failed. If I knew who the boss was, I'd hand in my notice. Being a parent is hard sometimes.

Do you ever feel like that about being my parent?

10

Standards of play

Tom comes bursting into the house with a package. 'I've got it!' he cries. 'Warren, I've got that toy!'

Warren is quickly at his side, pulling at the box. 'Is it "Bomb-burst"?' he asks, tearing at the carrier bag.

'Yes!' Tom tells him. 'Come on, let's get it set up.'

Warren has been waiting for this moment ever since he saw the toy advertised on television. Soon he and Tom have the contents of the box, all the interlocking bits of plastic and metal, strewn out over the floor and Tom is engrossed in the instructions. It's a bit fiddly, but soon he had it set up and he gives Warren the connecting lever.

'Give that a pull,' he says.

Warren gives the lever a mighty jerk and the whole structure that was put together by his dad disintegrates before their eyes – an explosion, just as advertised! Warren gives a yell of delight.

'Look, Mummy!' he calls.

And Kath comes to witness the next explosion. It's a pity that Warren can't help with the construction, but he gets great pleasure out of pulling the lever. It takes about ten minutes to construct the toy each time and less than

THE BOMB BURST TOY

a second to destroy it and, before long, Tom and Kath are both bored. So is Warren – between explosions. He goes off to find something else to do while his parents fit everything together again.

Then, in his excitement after one explosion, Warren stands on one of the plastic parts. There's a loud crunch that tells his parents that something vital is well and truly broken.

They look at each other and realise that they've just wasted a great deal of money.

Family values

Kath says, 'It wasn't worth as much as you paid for it.'

Tom replies, 'How was I to know it would be such tatty quality? And anyway the box didn't say that a child couldn't operate it alone.'

There's a long pause.

Kath says slowly, 'Why don't you pack it up again and pretend it was broken when you opened the box?'

Tom says nothing.

'It would serve them right for selling such stupid toys,' she says. 'And we'd get our money back.'

'It wouldn't be right,' he tells her. 'I should have looked more carefully before I bought it. Besides, what would it be teaching Warren?'

'He won't know,' she says. 'We'll buy him something else with the money.'

'It just doesn't seem right,' Tom said.

Warren is too young at three to understand the issues that Kath and Tom are discussing, but that really isn't the point.

What's at stake here is something vital to the family – whether or not honesty is the best policy. Or to put it more straightforwardly, are Tom and Kath going to live by God's standards or are they going to invent their own

– perhaps that it's all right to cheat as long as you get away with it or as long as there's a good outcome?

It may seem a trivial point in itself, involving only the cost of a toy, but the principles are most important. They are crucial to Warren, though he is totally ignorant of what's going on. This is going to affect his spiritual development.

Who is your God?

Tom and Kath are both Christians. Gita, who lives next door is not, but she has her own faith and beliefs. As Warren and Simran grow up they are going to be affected profoundly by what their parents believe.

It's not a matter of what they say about God. People can talk about God, teach about God, even say prayers to God, while still not living in the way he wants them to. Children are much more acute than some people give them credit for. They know the difference between words and actions. They quickly learn what really makes their parents tick. You may say that you obey God and want to do whatever he says, but if you always have something more important to do than worship, if you only ever think of yourself, if you openly do things that you believe are wrong, your words don't mean much to a child.

At this stage, and well into later childhood, children absorb the family beliefs. Whatever it is that we are truly devoted to, will become what our children believe in. We can't fool them.

If we get the greatest buzz in life out of impressing the neighbours with our new possessions, our children may well grow up to be materialists.

If we have devoted our lives to making easy money, how likely is it that they will grow up to be shallow and grasping?

If we live totally for football, dancing, music, theatre or ecology, our children will perceive that our particular interest is the most valuable thing in our lives. They too may come to share this consuming passion.

If the key to our lives is following Jesus, then there is a greater chance that our children will want to follow him too, to believe in him, serve him, love him and grow to know him. And this is what Christian parents want. It's no good just talking about it, though. Our values show in our actions. If Kath and Tom decide to deceive the toy shop into giving them their money back, they will be accepting a standard which isn't Christian. They will be allowing greed and self-interest to take precedence over Christ in their lives. If that is allowed to go on and God is pushed out of his rightful place in their home, it won't be good for Warren. He depends so much on their faith since he is too young to have faith independently.

It's serious, isn't it?

Taking the pressure off

On the other hand, it's quite a comfort to know that we don't have to do or be anything special to teach our children about God. Being a Christian means not living rigidly by a set of rules, but about having a relationship with God which transforms everything, even our moral behaviour.

And there aren't any rules about bringing up your child to have faith in God. We don't have to get them up early for family prayers. We don't have to devote Sunday afternoons to learning Bible verses. We don't have to sing religious songs all the time or try to mention God in every sentence.

Normal Christian living is enough. Of course we will talk about God sometimes and we will pray with our children, though not necessarily every day unless we want to. We will take them to church and read them Bible stories. What really matters, however, is to show our children by our lifestyle that Jesus is Lord. We may not talk about it much, but they will know.

They will know that they have received love, care and forgiveness from us. Our words about God and his love are backed up by our words and actions to them.

They will know that when we want to move house, for instance, we pray about it and ask God to show us whether it is what he wants. They will know that we save money so that we can give to, say, the earthquake appeal. They will know that we are willing to listen when a friend is in trouble. They will know that when someone lets us down, we forgive them and remain friends. They will know that we value the Bible and that we value prayer.

And they will want to be the same. They will grow up knowing Jesus because he has been part of the family from the start. For most there will never be a sudden 'conversion' experience of the type that Paul had on the road to Damascus (Acts 9:1–9). Instead, Jesus will be revealed to them more and more as they grow older, so that they will say, 'There never was a time when I didn't know Jesus.'

Many parents worry unduly about whether their children will 'become' Christians and anxiously watch their sons and daughters to see if there is any sign of faith. This can be very damaging for the children; it's a bit like pulling up the seedlings to see how they're growing. We need to relax more, not try to force our children to follow any particular way of life. We certainly can't influence them by giving them extra coaching in spiritual things!

We need to provide the right soil: a loving home where Christ is first in everything. Then stand back and watch them grow!

Is it just play?

Warren's choice of toy in the story that opened this chapter raises another matter important to childhood – play.

The expensive toy that Tom bought him was a failure because, although it looked good in the advertisements, there was actually nothing much for Warren to do. Such toys can be very exciting for a few minutes, but they soon end up in the corners of toy cupboards gathering dust. What we discover soon, hopefully before we have wasted too much money, is that the simpler toys are the better.

Warren has a bag of plain wooden bricks, six coloured plastic balls and a set of nesting baskets. One day, he built the bricks into four equal towers. He tried to place balls on the top of each tower, but they just rolled off. Then he had the idea of putting baskets on all the towers and happily discovered that he could make the balls stay on the towers by putting one in each basket. He realised he had two balls left over, so he built two more towers. By now he only had small baskets left and the balls wouldn't go right into them but perched on top. This seemed more satisfactory to him, so he changed the large baskets on the other four towers for smaller ones.

What did Warren learn by this play? There was certainly a lot of maths involved, though he wouldn't have recognised this. He was learning number, shape, size and volume at least. And he also enjoyed the achievement of being able to build, make decisions and reason by himself.

The next day Warren made the bricks into a square which he imagined as a house. The balls became people living in the house and he had to make a hole in the square for a door and each 'person' had to have a bed. The baskets came in handy here as the balls still had the habit of rolling off things. He pretended the Ball family's gran and grandad were coming to stay. They all had a meal at which the Boy Ball threw ice cream at Granny

Ball. He laughed a lot at this idea, but made sure the Boy Ball got told off for being so naughty.

In this game Warren was using his imagination. He was reflecting on his own family life and the things that happen to him at home, both the routines and the special occasions. He was able to develop an original, funny situation and he is developing his sense of justice.

Toys that encourage play

These simple toys provide almost endless play opportunities for Warren. The only limit is his imagination and ingenuity. The more he plays, the more creative he will become with the toys. Often children develop very complex games which involve parts of many toys, games and other household items. It does make a mess, but this is a disadvantage only for the parents. For the children, it's bliss! They can spend hours absorbed in their play and we need to allow them time and space for this. Their play can be destroyed if we're rushing them off to do other things. They may not even develop the ability to use their imagination properly in play – and that's when they start complaining of being bored!

The best toys are those that are most flexible. A doll which talks, cries, takes a bottle and wets her nappy leaves little to the imagination. Besides, it may become a nuisance to the child. Complex toys become a burden because they restrict creativity: there's a right and a wrong way to play with them. A rag doll, on the other hand, can be anything – baby, child, grown-up, animal, fairy, pillow – whatever the child wants. A train set that needs laying out and wiring up by an adult isn't much fun for a child. But there's endless amusement in a wooden train with engine and carriages to couple in various combinations and a wooden track that fixes together to form any layout the child wishes. Children also like cardboard boxes and tubes, lengths of fabric, wooden spoons, pebbles, feathers, scraps of paper, old clothes and hats . . . and anything else that we can safely give them.

There's a magical quality about children's play which we may remember from our own childhood. Sometimes it is described as a child's form of work. This idea does give some sense of its value, but play is far, far more than that. (If you are interested in this subject, read *Play is a Feeling* by Brenda Crowe.)

As they play, children learn and develop. They learn facts about the physical world, make sense of their everyday lives, work out problems, take on roles that they have seen others play, experiment, dream. Above all, successful, satisfying play builds a child's self-esteem.

REFLECTION

I remember a day when we had to keep clean and sit still because some important lady was coming to see our mum and dad. We tried to be good, though our arms and legs were aching to run around and stretch. But we couldn't behave because there was nothing to do, nothing to think, nothing – just sitting there looking at the important lady.

Soon the screaming in our heads came out of our mouths and we began to wriggle about without even meaning to. Mum and Dad said we were very, very bad. We believed them at the time, but now I wonder who was in the wrong that day. I don't think it was us children.

11

Three-legged stools

Warren's grandparents and other family members have been more important to him than he, at the age of four, realises. As they all live in other towns, he doesn't get to see them very much, though he really enjoys the occasional visits.

The wider family, however, has been a great support to Tom and Kath during the early years of Warren's life. It can be a lonely business bringing up children and even those parents who seem best at it have times of anxiety and doubt about what they're doing.

It's not always advice parents need at difficult times, though advice can sometimes be welcome. It's more a matter of having someone to talk to, someone who cares about you and your children, who understands that, when we say we have a problem, it doesn't mean that we're bad parents.

Grandparents and other close relatives can share, even if they live at a distance, those wonderful moments that happen in every family – the first smile, the funny things children say, the small achievements in their lives and many other details that seem insignificant to outsiders but are very precious to those who care about our children.

Finding support

Grandparents normally want to be involved as much as possible in the lives of their grandchildren but the fact is, for Tom and Kath, that it's not that straightforward. They're pleased that there's contact between their parents and Warren, of course, but they're anxious to prevent unwanted interference. So, while they listen to their parents' advice, they are careful not to follow it unthinkingly. After all, Warren is *their* responsibility and they both feel that they want to do things slightly differently from their own parents. They realise that they have to make up their own minds about how to deal with problems as they arise.

Three-legged stools are steady. Two-legged stools usually fall over and for some people who have children there is no family support. Being parents alone can be a very precarious task, especially for lone parents who don't even have a partner to share everything. Our society seems to portray an image of the ideal family as a unit that is totally independent of all support. It's not surprising that parents feel that they should be able to manage alone, without support and without advice.

This idea doesn't make sense any more than a two-legged stool makes sense! There's no other job in the world that is supposed to 'come naturally'. We don't put policemen out on the streets without any training or support. We don't let nurses go on to the wards without making sure that they have some basic knowledge and a great deal of supervision. Being a parent is no easy matter. There's a lot of basic training to do, some of which may happen during our own childhood at home, but much of which has to be learnt 'on the job'.

Parents need practical support too, someone to babysit,

an extra pair of hands when they or their children are sick, someone whom they can trust to look after the children in an emergency.

Parents need someone to talk to. We need to chat about what is going on. Does every child ask endless questions and how do we answer them? Is it usual for two year-olds to have bad dreams or is there something wrong with our son or daughter who has nightmares? Do other parents allow their toddlers into the bathroom with them or is this a bad idea? Should we treat boys and girls in different ways or will that just reinforce stereotypes? Such questions can be of great concern to parents. We all need other people to help us through the anxieties of parenthood and it's not good for anyone to be isolated.

That is why, in some areas, parent support groups have been formed. In some societies, parent support may happen naturally within the extended family and within the community. Today many people are isolated from their families and cannot easily get much help from their own neighbourhood nor even, sadly, from the church. Support groups or parentcraft courses are very welcome to those who attend. They are for ordinary parents and attendance doesn't imply failure to bring up our children properly.

Tom and Kath's experience

Before Warren's birth, Tom and Kath were both fairly involved in their local church. They attended regularly on Sundays and had joined a weekly study group. Kath helped with the youth group on Friday nights and Tom was out twice a week practising with the worship music band. They felt very much part of what was going on at church.

This all changed when Warren was born and their weekly routine was completely overturned. Even getting to church on Sunday mornings was difficult now that they had to fit it in between Warren's feed and rest times. Kath found she had little energy for the youth group and she also resented Tom being out for band practice, leaving her at home with Warren yet again. They gave up on the study group because the leader took no account of the agreed finishing time. This hadn't bothered them before, but now that they were having interrupted nights so often, they began to resent having to stay up late as well! On the other hand, they began to feel guilty that they had withdrawn from church life. Even finding time for personal prayer was hard. Tom especially felt bad about this. Sometimes when he had planned to spend some time alone with God, he found he just couldn't be bothered. He was too tired to make the effort.

Then they discovered what a great support their church could be. Before Warren arrived, they had enjoyed their work as part of the church community. Now they discovered a new way of belonging: they began to allow others to help them; they learnt that during the time when they were so very much tied up with their new baby, there were others around who would support them. Being less useful to the church didn't cut them off from it.

The church should be a family of those who follow Jesus, and part of being a family is the continuity of membership. You don't stop being part of a family when you're sick, have troubles or aren't able to contribute.

Nor, incidentally, does God reject us when we have difficulty finding time for devotions or worship. Many parents with small children have found it unhelpful to be pressurised in this area by those who have forgotten, or never knew, what it's like to be overwhelmed by exhaustion. Tom realised that his spiritual growth could continue throughout this demanding time of life, even without the formal 'quiet times' that he had insisted on before. He didn't stop praying, however, though his prayer became more spontaneous, which he began to see was actually quite a good thing!

As Warren grew a little older, Kath and Tom decided to form a group with a few other Christian parents. They meet just for an hour or so a week for prayer and to talk about what has happened to them as parents and what they are learning. They have both found that their relationship with God has developed as they have thought over their own parenting experiences and their experiences as children of God.

As everyone in the group has small children, they all know the importance of keeping to the agreed finishing time. Everyone understands if others are late or can't come at the last moment.

Kath and Tom have also discovered an older couple from the church who are delighted to be asked to babysit in the evenings, and they are very reliable. They feel that they are Warren's 'church grandparents' and Warren quickly began to recognise and trust them. They soon became very good friends and feel that they are benefitting from the arrangement too, since their own grandchildren live abroad. Both they and Kath and Tom enjoy having such close contact with others of a different generation in the church. It helps them to feel that the church is an all-age community, different generations enriching others.

It was this couple who suggested that Kath invite a friend to spend an evening a week with her to ease the time during Tom's absence for band practice. And, as Warren has grown older, they now often look after him during the day. The great thing about this arrangement, as far as Tom and Kath are concerned, is that it doesn't have to be made for only special reasons. Just having time to themselves is very valuable to them as a couple. They take care not to impose on their friends' generosity, though! They value their kindness too much to make unreasonable demands.

Finding time

Even so, Tom and Kath sometimes have to refuse when they are asked to take on new commitments. They could, if they tried, be out every night of the week and most of the weekend too, doing very valuable things in the church and the community.

It creates a great pressure on many families when much of the parents' energy is taken up with things outside the home. It can be a drain on our spiritual life when there's not enough time for the people who are most precious to us. In fact children can be left wondering how much their parents value them if the home is just a service station for parents with more important things to do elsewhere. In later years they will tend to treat the home in the same way.

Even fashionable 'quality' time isn't the whole answer for the children of busy parents. When parents can only spare short times of intense attention for their offspring, the children's self-esteem suffers. For, while they enjoy that special attention and the exciting treats, children also welcome peaceful, comforting times when the family is simply at home. They know that their parents are around even though nothing particular is happening. It's as though they are receiving a message that the parents really enjoy being with them. The parents are available, relaxed, at ease. Children gain a great feeling of security in the ordinariness of loving, everyday life, which gradually builds strength of character and spirit into young lives.

Though there must, of course, be times when parents are busy outside the home and also times when they are preoccupied by things which don't concern the family directly, children do have a right to be the centre of their parents' concern. The home should be the focus of every family member while the children are growing up. Around the home and the family children construct their images of themselves as worthy or as worthless people. How much happier our society would be if children grew up knowing that they were so lovable their parents 'wasted' time doing nothing but just being with them!

To find this kind of time in a busy society, parents may have to ask themselves questions about their priorities – and that won't always be easy, especially for people who work full-time, those who have other unavoidable commitments or those who like having lots of interests outside the home.

It's both the privilege and the responsibility of parents to be 'pictures of Christ' to their children, just as Jesus is our picture of God. What we know about God, we know because we have seen it in Jesus and, in the same way, what our children know about God, they have learnt from us, not just through our words but through our characters, behaviour and attitudes. This is an awesome responsibility and one which we can't carry out on our own. How much we need the help of the Holy Spirit!

So, what kind of God do we want children to believe in as they grow up – one who is able to spare time for them occasionally or one who enjoys lavishing his attention on them because he loves them so much? Let's *show* our children just how much God really does love them. *His* attention is something on which they can always rely.

REFLECTION

'Lord, you have examined me and you know me.
You know everything I do; from far away you
understand all my thoughts.
You see me, whether I am working or resting;
you know all my actions.

Even before I speak, you already know what I
will say. You are all round me on every side;
you protect me with your power.

Your knowledge of me is too deep; it is beyond
my understanding.'
Psalm 139:1–6

12

The intruder

Finding time for Warren becomes a pressing issue for Tom and Kath when his sister, Melanie, is born.

They thought they had prepared Warren pretty well. They involved him in all the preparations so that he could feel part of what was going on as he helped to fix up the spare room for the baby. They looked out stories about children having baby brothers or sisters and made sure that he saw lots of babies so that he might know what to expect.

The first couple of weeks went quite well. Warren showed a lot of interest in Melanie and was helpful in small ways. He even enjoyed all the visits from friends and relatives to see the baby. Some of them brought presents for the big brother as well as for the baby, so it was a bit like an extra birthday for him.

Now the novelty seems to have worn off and things don't look quite so good. Melanie suffers from colic and demands a lot of attention. Warren is being very difficult. He is irritable and won't settle to play as he used to. Nor, suddenly, will he allow other people to look after him. If he falls over or bumps his head, he reacts like a much

smaller boy and cries pitifully until someone comes to comfort him. He has gone back to sucking his thumb.

It doesn't seen fair to Tom and Kath that he is behaving like this. It feels as though they've got *two* demanding babies in the family instead of one. Both of them vie for attention all day long.

The intruder

Look at it from Warren's point of view. Can you imagine how you would feel if your partner brought home somebody else one day? 'It's OK,' they might say, 'I'll still love you just the same.' But then your partner begins to spend hours and hours with this other person. And, just as you get a moment's attention, the intruder calls for something and your partner runs off to attend to the other person again.

It must feel a bit like that to Warren. He has lost his exclusive status. Now there is someone else sharing his home, his parents and his right to their attention. No wonder he feels acute jealousy.

He didn't know that it would be like this when he happily prepared for Melanie's arrival. He may not even have realised that she would stay so long. Now it seems that she is going to be around permanently. What can he do?

Melanie is a baby and she gets lots of attention. Perhaps if he behaves like a baby, he will regain his status and Melanie will disappear. This is very difficult and upsetting for Warren because, while he likes Melanie and enjoys having a baby around, he also feels murderously angry about her and wants to get rid of her.

A jealous child needs help. It can be hard for parents to admit that their older children feel bad about the new baby, especially when they have done everything they can to make things easy. However, pretending that it isn't happening won't help the situation. Older children can be left with very negative feelings about themselves if they are not helped at this crucial stage in their development.

Someone special

For a time Warren will need to know that he is someone very special to his parents. They can allow him to 'visit' being a baby again and give him comfort when he hurts himself and not nag him when he sucks his thumb.

On the other hand, they will want to show him the benefits of being a 'big' boy. He can be reminded of all the good things that happen to him because he is no longer a baby: he can have a special outing, he can choose his favourite stories and games, he can stay up after Melanie is in bed.

Kath and Tom can be careful to make time for him too, time that won't be interrupted by Melanie's needs. They can ask friends and relatives to pay as much attention to Warren as to the baby and they won't say things which will give him false expectations. For instance, there's no point in saying, 'Soon you'll be able to play with Melanie.' His timescale is more immediate than theirs and he will get fed up waiting for Melanie to do something more than smile and wave her arms and legs!

Above all, Kath and Tom can allow Warren to show his anger at what has happened. Of course he mustn't hurt Melanie or do any serious damage. There may be occasions, though, when his feelings show themselves unexpectedly. They are real and shouldn't be played down. In a way, it is right for Warren to feel bad about the intruder in his home. His parents can help him by understanding what he feels, acknowledging that he does feel cross and giving him a legitimate way of expressing it, eg pounding some dough or going for a puddle stamp.

It would be sad if Warren felt that his bad feelings made him unacceptable. He isn't being 'naughty' or unreasonable because his behaviour is difficult. He is learning how to deal with jealousy and there's a confusing mix of love and hatred inside him. He still has a great longing to be loved. If his parents are always showing their disapproval of his babyish and demanding behaviour, Warren may get the message that they no longer love him, even though nothing is further from the truth. Of course they do still love him, but it will be hard for Warren to understand this if the only attention he gets is irritable or nagging. He needs extra support at this time, lots of patient understanding and masses of reassurance!

Fairness or equality?

Melanie is different from Warren right from the start. She's a fretful baby but doesn't like to be handled too much. Warren, on the other hand, was happiest when he was being cuddled and was generally much more relaxed.

Kath and Tom often think of the early days with Warren when they used to enjoy picking him up and rocking him to sleep in their arms. Melanie will have none of that! She cries to be put down in her cot or pram and, if she gets too much stimulation, she can't seem to settle for a long time afterwards. Her parents are having to re-learn much of what they had begun to take for granted with Warren.

Kath and Tom are getting the message loud and clear: Melanie is her own person, not a carbon copy of her big brother.

They had planned to treat the two children entirely equally. Warren had lots of individual attention when he was a baby and so Melanie was to get the same. The trouble is that Melanie doesn't want to have rattles waved at her so much. She enjoys being talked to for only so long before she begins to give the message that she's had enough. She spends much longer on her own.

Naturally her parents feel a bit guilty about this, but the fact is that it's Melanie who is setting the pace. Tom and Kath could decide to be rigid about this and give Melanie everything Warren had in exactly the same way. This would be treating the children equally, but would it be fair?

Because Melanie is an individual, she needs to be treated as such. She is not Warren and the differences between the children will become more and more apparent as they grow older. There will be situations when something which is fair and right for Warren will be wrong and totally unfair for Melanie (and vice versa), not because they are a different sex but because they are different characters.

Warren was ready to go to playgroup from the age of three, but it may be wrong for Melanie to be taken along at the same age for the sake of equality. It may be that she would be happier to stay at home until she is ready to deal with children in larger groups. Going to playgroup before she is confident about playing with other children in ones and twos might impede her social development rather than advance it.

A word of caution here: parents are often hard-pressed and can't give as much time as they would like to weighing up how to treat children as individuals in this way. Sometimes other considerations have to be given priority, which doesn't matter so long as the children know that they are equal yet different.

Growing in faith

In the same way, parents need to be fair to their children as they encourage them to grow in faith. One child might enjoy talking about Jesus and ask lots of questions. Another might enjoy occasional Bible stories but not want to talk about what she has heard. One child might like going to the children's group at church and come home singing all the songs and talking about God. Another might prefer to stay with her parents and enjoy sitting through an adult service.

There are many ways of learning about God and getting to know him. There are probably no two people in the world who have exactly the same experience of him. So we shouldn't expect two children, even from the same family, to follow the same path in their faith development. At the earliest stages of faith, it's a matter of what children experience that is crucial. Who can tell what a child is really understanding as he soaks in the atmosphere of home and church?

We can't assume that one kind of expression of faith is better for children than another. A child who talks about Jesus, can remember Bible stories and asks lots of questions about God is no more or less 'Christian' than one who silently gazes at a flower, lost in wonder at its beauty. Both are experiencing God. Both are getting to know him and both are accepted by him by grace.

Our task as parents is to enable children to get to know God. We can't force it, but we can encourage it. (Some practical ideas appear in the final chapter of this book.) Our children will react in different ways, of course, and we shouldn't always be looking for verbal 'proof' that they are developing their own relationship with God. Sensitive parents will know, without a word being spoken, that God is at work in their children's lives. If that is so, there's nothing much to worry about!

REFLECTION

I heard you say, 'Jean is a Christian. She gave her
heart to Jesus last week. John isn't a Christian
yet, but we are praying for him.'
Well, it sounded funny that Jean had given her
heart away. I saw her in the bath and you
couldn't see where they'd taken her heart out
through her chest.
I don't think I want to be a Christian if that's
what it means. And I didn't like how it felt
when you said that. Does it mean you love Jean
more than me now? Something about what
Jean did made you happy. Am I making you sad?
Do you think I don't love Jesus? Is that what
it is? Perhaps I don't love him in the right way.
I wish I could understand what it all means.
All I know is – when they sing those songs
about Jesus, I feel happy to be his friend. Happy
right down inside.

13

Just parents

Now that there are two children in the family, life has changed for Tom and Kath again, but it will always be changing. Family life is never stagnant. There's always someone growing – children and adults alike. There's always movement – children making further steps towards independence and interdependence, and parents adjusting as they allow their children to move on. There's always gain – members of the family arriving or developing. And there's always loss – people leaving or dying or growing away.

The reality is that, no matter how we try, we cannot keep our children as they are forever. Nor can we fossilise our families at a certain stage to prevent change. Family life is dynamic. It never settles down. It always brings new challenges.

It's a bit like a spiral. Family life keeps turning. The first time round you're a child at the hub of the wheel, cared for and surrounded by the older generations. The next time around, you may be a parent with responsibilities to your children and to older generations. On the next turn, your children have left home and are maybe bringing up their own children, but you may also be caring for an older generation. Finally, you are dependent again, perhaps on your own children. And the spiral turns on.

Looking to the future

Having a long-term perspective can be important even when our children are small. Their leaving seems a very long time ahead but it must happen one day. In fact we don't want them to stay forever. Having a middle-aged son or daughter still living at home is not something most people would appreciate.

And because we know they're going to grow up, we want to do the very best we can for our children. Let's examine what this might mean.

'We want our children to be independent.' So we encourage them to learn the basic skills of human life. We show them how to get on well with others. We give them chances to make their own decisions. We give them greater and greater space to take risks, even if that means making mistakes.

'We want our children to be happy.' So we surround them with love so that they grow up confident of their own worth. We teach them to value other people more than material things. We show them how and when to put their rights on one side in favour of others, and how and when to insist on their rights.

'We want our children to know right from wrong.' So, instead of letting wrong choices appear to be attractive and forbidden, we demonstrate that we can choose to do what is right joyfully. We don't hide from them the harm that can come from making wrong choices. We don't expect them to make moral decisions beyond their abilities but

according to their age and stage of development. We don't confuse or irritate them by moralising about their behaviour at every opportunity. We don't condemn them for making mistakes. We positively encourage them to make right choices, even when that is hard.

'We want our children to be kind, loving, forgiving, honest and truthful.' So, we're *kind* to them and don't take advantage of their weakness to bully them in word or deed. We demonstrate that we *love* them even when their behaviour isn't lovely. We *forgive* them even when they have hurt us badly or shown us up in public. We don't keep mentioning the times when they were wrong. We are *honest* with them even when it means admitting our mistakes to them. We always tell them the *truth* and reward their courage in telling the truth when lying would have been easier.

'We want our children to be Christians.' So, we provide them with a home life which is Christian. We try to make God's values our values. We try to reflect God's parenting love to them, not just on special occasions, but every day. We invite Jesus to be one of the family and honour him in everything we do. Well, that's what we aim for, but . . .

Parents who fail

We can't be good parents all the time, as we have seen. We can only aspire to do our best, and we shouldn't be dismayed if we make mistakes or fail to reach the standards we have set ourselves. Even when things go wrong, children can learn positive lessons if we're willing to admit mistakes.

Let's take an example. One day, Tom was looking after the children. It was nearly Christmas and there were some presents for the children hidden in the wardrobe. When Tom opened the wardrobe, he found that the presents had been tampered with. Several of the wrappings had been torn. He was very upset. It felt that Christmas had been spoilt and he thought he knew who had done it.

Warren, he felt, was old enough to know better. He called his son in and confronted him with the evidence. Warren burst into tears, but Tom refused to comfort him. He sent him to bed and insisted that he stay there for the rest of the morning. At lunch time, Warren was very subdued, but Tom was still angry at what had happened, so there was no reconciliation.

When Kath came home later in the day, Tom told her the story, including what he had done to Warren 'to teach him not to do it again'.

'Oh Tom,' Kath said, 'that wasn't fair. Melanie got into the wardrobe yesterday while I wasn't looking and ripped all the paper off before I could stop her. It wasn't Warren at all.'

Tom was clearly in the wrong over this incident. He had made false assumptions and Warren had suffered because of it. Warren was helpless in this situation and couldn't work out logically that Tom's displeasure wasn't justified, so he couldn't defend himself against the accusation.

There are two things Tom could do now. He could protect himself, blame Kath for not telling him the full story beforehand or blame Warren for not standing up for himself. He could make excuses and say he was tired and it wasn't right that he should be left alone with the children after a hard week at work.

On the other hand, he could admit that he was wrong. That means taking responsibility for what happened. He could say sorry to Warren and explain that he had made a big mistake. He could make it clear that Warren wasn't to blame at all. If this happens, some positive things could come out of Tom's failure to be a good parent. The peace of the home would be restored, and Warren would learn how to say sorry. He might also learn what it means to forgive. His love and respect for his father could grow. However, none of these things will happen if Tom is unable to admit responsibility.

And Kath has a part to play to. It would be easy for her to play a game of one-up-man-ship. She could remind Tom endlessly of the incident whenever anything goes wrong in the family. Tom's failure puts her in a better light since she would obviously never make such a stupid mistake – or so she may think.

Yet she would be wrong to do this. Being parents isn't a competition to see who is better than the other. It's about working together and relying on each other's strengths. Fault-finding between couples leads to a lot of distress. Sometimes people feel so demoralised when this is always happening to them that they give up altogether and leave their partner to get on with the job of parenting alone.

Kath's prompt forgiveness is as necessary to the family's peace as Tom's acknowledgement that he made a mistake. It makes it more likely that next time *she* makes a mistake, Tom will be able to forgive her!

Family rituals

Rituals add richness to life. We are surrounded by human rituals from the simple, like the formality of shaking hands when meeting a stranger, to the complex, like the state opening of Parliament. In family life, rituals are important too. Children learn to rely on the daily, weekly and annual happenings that mark their lives.

Christian parents want to include God in their family lives and so it isn't surprising that they often look for things to do with their children which will mark the presence of God among them. It doesn't mean that he isn't there already. It simply means that they want to acknowledge him in some way.

Read Bible stories. We need to have well-told versions of suitable Bible stories if they are to be helpful rather than confusing. Bible language, even in modern versions, isn't easily understood by small children and some of the stories need a much more sophisticated understanding of the world than any under-five is likely to have.

Take children to church. Many parents feel that their children won't be welcome in church in case they make a noise or run around. Yet many churches are pleased to see parents with small children and people are quite understanding about a little noise. As a matter of fact, children who attend church from an early age are likely to be less disruptive than those who are only there occasionally. They tend to absorb the atmosphere of worship and know instinctively when to be quiet. However, there should be good provision for small children, including creche facilities for babies and toddlers – these are the signs of a church that really cares about families with young children. But there should also be times when people of all ages worship together. When this happens, children have the opportunity to grow up being part of the worshipping community and don't feel side-lined.

Say thanks at meal times. There's no need to make this custom too rigid, but it's good to remember that God provides us with the food we eat. Our children will enjoy saying a simple prayer of thanks, even if it's said just once a day or once a week.

Celebrate Christian festivals. Do something special at Christmas and Easter to remind each other of the Christian significance of the festival. This could be as simple as gathering together on Christmas Eve for a few minutes to light a candle and sing a carol about the birth of Jesus. At Easter you could arrange some flowers in a special vase to remind yourselves that Jesus is alive. Tell the children why we give Easter eggs to each other.

Take time to wonder. Life can be so busy that we fail to notice what's going on around us. So, make time to gaze at a spider's web, look at reflections in puddles, run in the wind, watch raindrops on windows, follow the progress of a snail crawling so slowly across the ground, notice shadows and shade. These activities, simple though they are, put us and our children in touch with the wonder of God's creation. Romans 1:19–20 indicates that observing the natural world is one way in which God reveals himself to us.

Play Christian music. Don't go for the trite messages of much children's music but for something which has worship and reverence at its heart. Children may learn a great deal from the words and the music, but don't overdo it! There are other kinds of music, too, with their own appeal and value.

Say daily prayers. This can mean a familiar prayer at the beginning or the end of the day. Anything more formal might become hard to keep going as children grow older or get tiresome to have to organise every day. You could make your own book of prayers, adding to it when you feel inspired. The best prayers are those which talk to God in simple, everyday language about things that matter to the whole family. It can be a help to have a couple of standard prayers, like the ones below, that the children can learn by repeated use. The children like the familiarity of the words and can develop their own private prayers from them. Parents may not be able to find or think up new prayers for each occasion, so appreciate a known prayer, especially if it can easily be adapted to fit the events of the day.

A PRAYER FOR THE MORNING

Our Father God, at the start of this new day, we
thank you for all the things that we will do.
Thank you for the clothes we put on.
Thank you for the home where we live.
Thank you for the food we eat.
Thank you for the people we will meet.
Thank you that you will be with us every
moment of today.
Amen.

A PRAYER FOR THE EVENING

Dear Jesus, you have been with us all the day.
Thank you for the good things about today,
especially . . .
We are sorry if we did things today which hurt
other people or made them sad.
Now as we get ready to go to sleep, help us to
remember that you love us and never leave us.
Thank you, Jesus.
Amen.

And finally . . .

Your children will be small for only a short time, though it may not seem so at present! In only a few years your family will be moving on to a new stage, so it's important to make the most of the present.

Without doubt, having small children is tiring, perplexing and often mundane. You will probably never feel wistful about sleepless nights, trying to keep up with a toddler or reading the same book to your child for the umpteenth time! On the other hand, there are joys and opportunities at this stage which will never occur again. These early years are most important for our children, the foundation of their physical, emotional and spiritual well-being. When we feel tired, perplexed or bored, remember that what we are doing *is* vital. If parents were paid a fair rate for the job, we would all be millionaires!

This is a time of rapid growth for our children, as we know. It's also a time when we can grow too. Being a parent is an education. It presents opportunities for personal development, for instance to become more selfless, sensitive and self-confident. It's an opportunity to develop a new phase of marriage and to explore the possibilities of family life. It's a creative time when you can take risks together and begin to set the unique tone of your family.

There is no 'right' way of bringing up a family (though there are 'wrong' ways). God has given us endless possibilities, and so long as we keep him central to our way of life and are sensitive to each other's needs, we are free to explore new territory together. We can hold on to what's been good in the past, the good things we learnt from our own parents. But your family with its unique combinations of personalities has never happened before. With God's help, and with Christ as an example, you have the opportunity to build something original, fresh and good. May you enjoy doing so!

125

A PRAYER FOR FAMILIES

Lord Jesus, in times of joy, may we thank you
together;
in times of sorrow may be find your comfort in
each other;
in times of success may we glow with a generous
pride that warms everyone;
in times of failure may we forgive each other and
receive a new start from you.
We ask you to be part of our family, in our
home, with us wherever we are. Make it possible
for others to come to know you because they see
how much you mean to us.

Courses for parents published in the UK:

Help! I'm a parent, Church Pastoral Aid Society
What can a parent do?, Veritas, Family Caring Trust
Faith in the family, David Durston, The Bible Society